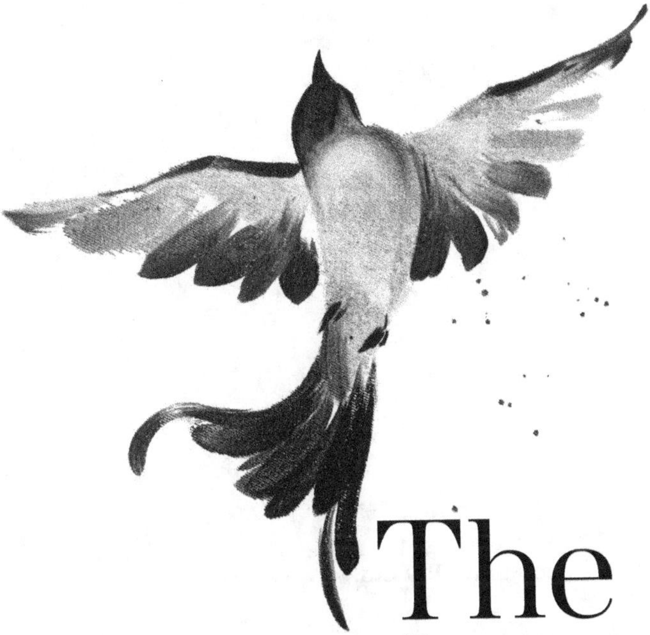

The Eighteen Point Five

18.5% of Australians live with a disability. We are 25 of them and share our stories.

A book by Eighteen Point Five Pty Ltd
Concept by John Duthie
Editing by Beverley Streater

Copyright 2020 Eighteen Point Five Pty Ltd.

All rights reserved. No portion of this book may be reproduced, stored in a retrieval system, or transmitted in any form or by any means—electronic, mechanical, photocopy, recording, scanning, or other—except for brief quotations in critical reviews or articles, without the prior written permission of the publisher.

Published by Eighteen Point Five Pty Ltd.

ISBN 978-0-6489037-0-3 (printed book)
ISBN 978-0-6489037-1-0 (electronic book)
ISBN 978-0-6489037-2-7 (audio book)

A catalogue record for this book is available from the National Library of Australia

The Eighteen Point Five

This book is dedicated to the 18.5% of Australians
living with a disability or disorder.

And the team members who made this book possible
One project manager
Twenty-five contributors
Ten writers
Five proof-readers
An editor
Supporters
Advisors
Helpers

And the sponsors who generously provided
funding for the book project.

Foreword

JOHN DUTHIE WAS WATCHING HIS TWO CHILDREN PARTICIPATE in a sports day. A tree branch severed his spine at the chest level and he now lives with an SCI (Spinal Cord Injury).

John read twenty-five memoirs of living with a disability and became aware that unless you were well known, you wouldn't get published. The solution was to produce a book of twenty-five stories, featuring people living their lives with a disability. John didn't know who would be interested, or how to run a book project, or how to publish a book.

He planned the project, created a website and social media, and established a vision: 'To encourage people with a disability, and to increase the knowledge and understanding of disability in the community'. The project asked for contributions, and many of the storytellers wrote the stories themselves. Others required help. The search for additional writers, proof-readers and an editor commenced.

Team members came from four states of Australia, with an international flair from people in Indonesia, the UK and the USA. The twenty-five people featured all have their ups and downs, and one conclusion comes from each account: living with a disability is not easy, but people with disabilities can enjoy life and achieve goals.

It took over two years from the initial idea until the book was complete.

The book title, *The Eighteen Point Five*, is based upon 18.5% of the population within Australia having a disability or disorder.

Contents

Chapter 1	*Portrait of An Author (or My Life in Words)* by John Rynn and Judith Buckingham	1
Chapter 2	*High-Viz Happiness* by Michael Kuhn and May-Kuan Lim	13
Chapter 3	*Alice's Journey* by Alice Waterman and Emily Woolford	27
Chapter 4	*Struggling with Faith* by John Duthie	35
Chapter 5	*Living in Adelaide As a Couple with Disability* by Faisal Rusdi and edited by Marie Doener	49
Chapter 6	*See the Real Me* by Jacy Arthur and Diana von der Borch-Garden	63
Chapter 7	*Do You Ever Feel Like You Just Don't Fit In?* by Phillippa Smoker	71
Chapter 8	*Our Journey with James* by Cristina Lantican Rodert	79
Chapter 9	*The Obstacle Course* by Ross Hill-Brown and John Francis	93
Chapter 10	*Living with Deafblindness* by Linda Fistonich and Valerie Everett	111
Chapter 11	*A NEWS-Worthy Knock-On* by Jonathan Nguyen and Chantel Bongiovanni	121
Chapter 12	*Will You Die Before Your Death?* by Tracey Meg and May-Kuan Lim	131

Chapter 13	*What We're Wheelie Like* by Gail Miller	145
Chapter 14	*Intermissioned. Take 1* by Neville Hiatt.	153
Chapter 15	*Balancing Act* by Kathryn Hall and Rachel Mann	163
Chapter 16	*Behind Closed Doors* by Melinda Jones and David Wayne Wilson	173
Chapter 17	*Deaf, Blind and On the Catwalk* by Vanessa Vlajkovic	183
Chapter 18	*Save The Drama for The Llama* by Zia Westerman and Pamela Farley	191
Chapter 19	*Bee-Longing* by Bee Williamson	203
Chapter 20	*How to Be Beautiful* by Grant Lock	213
Chapter 21	*A Treasure Hunter* by Alex Blackmore and Nadja Fernandes	219
Chapter 22	*Daring to Dream* by Mary Albury and Valerie Everett	227
Chapter 23	*My Life with Huntington's Disease* by Ben Wilson	239
Chapter 24	*Redlegs and Family* by Rick Neagle and Marie Doerner	247
Chapter 25	*Losing Sight, Gaining Insight* by Nadja Fernandes	255

PLATINUM SPONSOR

Help at Home Inc.

helpathomeinc.com.au

Help At Home is a charitable not-for-profit organisation that was created in 1991 by a small group of dedicated volunteers who recognised the growing need to provide in-home support to people living with a disability and the elderly in their local community.

Since then Help At Home has grown to employ over 160 staff and is committed to providing personalised support services throughout metropolitan South Australia. Help At Home is a registered NDIS provider and staff are screened, trained and accredited.

Help At Home offers a wide range of services to assist clients—from younger people with a disability through to the aged—to achieve their goals and maintain their independence and quality of life in their own home. We listen to our clients and aim to match support workers to their goals and needs. Our dedicated caring team provide a high level of planning and support to our clients and their support staff.

Help At Home provides quality customised services including assistance with self-care, respite, social and community supports, life skills, domestic assistance, overnight care and support coordination.

Help At Home understands and respects everyone's individuality and we believe empathy, compassion, integrity, and commitment are essential values. The people we assist are an inspiration and enrich our lives as well.

We are proud to sponsor the Eighteen Point Five book project.

GOLD SPONSORS

Brazier Mobility

braziermobility.com.au

Brazier Mobility, located in Adelaide, has helped people with disability get out of their homes and into the community for over thirty years. We help people get into cars, get their things into cars, as well as drive themselves. Every customer has different needs which means that every job we do is unique to that individual. Everything begins with a process of getting to know our customer; exploring the options and arriving at the best solution possible.

We also perform complete vehicle wheelchair accessible vehicle conversions for community organisations and individuals. These can range from large buses to smaller family cars.

At Brazier Mobility, we work closely with occupational therapists, healthcare professionals, physiotherapists, NDIS personnel and support workers. It's a team exercise that relies on honest and open communication.

We are extremely proud of our reputation for delivering high quality solutions in a reasonable timeframe, and at a fair price.

The ability to travel independently is becoming more and more important in people's everyday lives. We believe that having disability should never take away a person's ability to travel. We work tirelessly to turn this dream into a reality.

Visit our website or call us on 1800 BRAZIER (1800 272 943).

Beverley Streater

(editor)
www.linkedin.com/in/beverley-streater/

During a long career in human services, Beverley transitioned from face to face service delivery in aged and disability services, to coordinating services, managing teams, and finally providing strategic advice and communications to senior personnel.

Her areas of expertise include writing (content, correspondence), editing (both structural and copy-editing), strategic planning, complaints management, quality assurance, customer service, administrative tasks, office management, logistics, leadership, training, coaching.

Beverley brings these skills into play as a freelance editor, offering honest and reasoned feedback to authors in a gentle and constructive way. As an Associate Member of the Institute of Professional Editors, she works with authors of both fiction and non-fiction manuscripts. The opportunity to broaden her reading while assisting writers in expressing themselves effectively has resulted in a successful win/win formula.

In recent years, she became aware of the needs of older women approaching the transition to retirement, which inspired me to set up an interactive and resourceful blog called Classic Women.

She currently combines her contribution as a volunteer in her community (Justice of the Peace, Secretary of the Gold Coast Writers' Association, committee member of Palm Beach Creative Stitchers), alongside her freelance editing work.

Wright Evans Partners

wepartners.com.au

Wright Evans Partners is a chartered accounting firm based in Adelaide. Commencing in 2008, we are a successful, respected and innovative firm with a fresh approach to the accounting and business services industry.

We promise exceptional service without losing sight of the personal touches. With a comprehensive accounting team, specialised superannuation division, internal financial planners and brokers, we provide a complete "one stop shop" for all your financial needs, both as an individual or business.

We are proud sponsors of the Flinders Medical School and the Adelaide University Dental School and have been offering industry specific services and advice to the medical and dental professions for over a decade.

Marie Doerner

welearnwomen.org

FOR THE PAST FORTY YEARS, MARIE HAS LIVED IN THE USA with annual visits to her hometown, Adelaide. Life went on, she raised four children and began a career teaching adults with disabilities to read, write and do math. Marie is currently a learning disability specialist for San Diego Continuing Education.

In an effort to encourage writing, she had her students submit writing for publication. That is when she became involved with WE LEARN and their annual journal of writing by learners in literacy programs. Now in its 15th edition, Women's Perspectives motivates students to become enthusiastic writers.

Marie's two worlds converged when she heard about 18.5. On her next visit to Adelaide, she met with John and volunteered as a writer and proofreader. She has worked with several team members to write, edit, discuss and fine tune writing to move the project forward.

In San Diego, Movement Be says, 'Tell your story before they do'. This book, *Eighteen point five percent*, does just that. People with disabilities telling their lived stories. Real people with real stories.

Waterman Property Advocates

watermanpa.com.au

WATERMAN
Property Advocates

Adelaide Born & Bred. For Property.

We're here for you.

Our knowledge means you will get the right agent, for the right price, who will do the right thing by you. With more than 30 years' experience we have intimate knowledge of all aspects of buying, selling, renting, clearing and preparing real estate for any purpose.

We work for you.

SACARE

sacare.com.au

SACARE is a South Australian family owned and operated business dedicated to providing high quality housing, care and allied-health services for people with a complex disability. For more details visit our website.

SILVER SPONSORS

Serenity Homes

serenityhomes.com.au

Serenity Homes Pty Ltd, established in March 2001 by business owners Gary and Jennifer Barnes, is a family-owned luxury custom builder based in South Australia, and continues to remain under their inspirational leadership.

Choosing to only build a select number of homes a year, each project is a collaboration built on integrity, honesty and open dialogue with clients.

Serenity Homes caters for both the new custom built home market and premium home additions/renovations market.

We enjoy what we do, and this is reflected in the homes we create; building all styles of homes including traditional, classic and modern contemporary.

Alive and not Kicking

alive-and-not-kicking.com

Alive and not Kicking is an appropriate name for a memoir about paralysis resulting from an accident.

John Duthie was supporting his children at a school sports day, and a tree fell on him. He wasn't expected to survive and spent thirty days in ICU. After a year in rehabilitation, including the onset of chronic pain, he returned home and faced many challenges. It included separation, divorce, bullying and attempted suicide.

However, John is now loving life, achieving goals, having fun, being a dad, swimming, driving, riding, while dealing with the realities of living with an acquired disability.

And he is alive (and not kicking).

Xtracare Equipment

xtracareequipment.com.au

Xtracare Equipment is a family owned and run business that has been helping people find the right assistive technology since 1995. We are an NDIS approved service provider who go above and beyond to find equipment solutions that enable our clients to meet and exceed their goals.

Our area of expertise lies specifically with custom-made manual and sports wheelchairs, power wheelchairs, positioning and pressure management, paediatric rehabilitation equipment and equipment modifications.

Let's Remember This

letsrememberthis.com

John Francis is a Melbourne-based writer and videomaker. He specialises in telling people's personal histories, in print and in video and podcast documentaries.

Each of us has a unique story to tell. As we get older, we become aware that our life experiences have value for our children, and their children, and so on. John's job is to present life histories so that they 'come alive', and 'connect' with those who come after us, those whose lives, inevitably, are so different.

Spring Studio Melbourne

springstudio.com.au

Based in Melbourne, Spring Studio provides high quality audio and video recording and production.

With thirty-seven years in Australia, Harry Williamson brings an experienced and collaborative spirit to each new project.

We also record audio books for Amazon, create original music and backing tracks, and manufacture sound booths for the ABC, the army, universities and private clients

Please get in touch if you have a creative project you'd like to discuss. harry@springstudio.com.au

WheelchairJohn

wheelchairjohn.com

WheelchairJohn is a bad way of describing who I am, as it places emphasis on my mobility device. I am John Duthie, and I have a spinal injury which causes me to use a wheelchair. However, WheelchairJohn is easy to remember and sounds better than JohnWheelchair, or JohninaWheelchair or other combinations.

At age forty-four, I almost died and acquired a complete SCI (Spinal Cord Injury) at the chest level. I developed chronic pain, and a few times, I considered death a better alternative. Now I believe life is still worth living, although it has many challenges.

My blog shares my life with an acquired disability.

Rundle Blinds & Curtains

rundleblinds.luxaflex.com.au

Since the 1950s, the family-owned and operated Rundle Blinds & Curtains has custom-made top quality curtains & blinds. We've moved from manufacturing our products to selling the world-leading LUXAFLEX window fashions range. As one of the biggest curtain retailers in the state, we offer on-trend styling solutions for your home.

Our focus is to provide a seamless customer experience with the product, install and design experts to help you every step of the way. Our showroom in Kings Park offers the opportunity to see and experience our full range of products, with professional advice to help you create the perfect ambience for your home.

Hannah, Cristina, James and Kym Rodert

Our family lives a challenging yet fulfilling and rewarding life. James, our son was born with Down Syndrome and has been diagnosed with autism. In addition, James is speech and hearing impaired.

Although he hasn't spoken a word in his life, we understand James well. Our chapter aims to raise awareness and understanding of people living with multiple disabilities and special needs. We welcome you to read 'Our Journey with James'.

Aspect Conveyancing

aspectconveyancing.com

Aspect Conveyancing have worked in the property industry for over twenty-five years. We specialise in land development and handle all aspects of both residential and commercial conveyancing. Aspect Conveyancing is a newly established firm with a fresh approach to conveyancing. Our personalised service and expertise takes the stress out of your property transaction.

At Aspect Conveyancing we can assist with the following services: contract and pre-purchase advice; residential; private contracts; Form 1 preparation; matrimonial and defacto transfers; family transfers; deceased estates; land divisions (both Torrens and Community); specialising in land development.

Stephan Siciliano - Ray White Norwood

raywhitenorwood.com.au/agents/stefan-siciliano/72489

Reliable, likable and always available, Stefan Siciliano knows no boundaries to service and commits 24/7 to his real estate career, and your results. He puts in the long hours, putting valuable hours back in your pocket.

That's what *real* real estate agents do. He is also alert to the subtle shifts in market turns, and he converts data into opportunity.

Backed by Ray White's global audience, the largest database of clients throughout Australasia, and its tight grip on the luxury property market, you win.

BUYING THE BOOK FOR OTHER PEOPLE

Did you enjoy the book?
Would you like to gift the book to your employees,
clients, neighbours, friends, family or other people?
If the answers are **yes** and **yes**, we can deliver
the books to you, around Australia, for as low as
$9.70* a book. A large discount on the RRP.

eighteenpointfive.com.au/gifts

(* The cost varies with the number of books ordered.
Visit our website for the latest information and prices.)

ONE

Portrait of An Author (or My Life in Words)

by John Rynn and Judith Buckingham

I WAKE FROM NO DREAMS TO A DAY OF DREAMS.

It's not Christmas, not my birthday. Those come every year. This is special.

A soft knock from outside. A mop of grey hair around the door: my carer.

'Today's the day, John. Excited?'

What do you think? If I could, I would be dancing around the room.

Beside me on my bedside table lies a book, an advance copy of *You Only Want Me For My Mind, and Other Bedtime Stories*, by

John Rynn[1]. So far it has only been read by me, my family and close friends. Today ... my story, my book, is going to be launched into the world. I am now a published author.

Most writers who complete a book never get published.

Most writers who publish do not get worldwide distribution.

Most writers do not have athetoid quadriplegia - a form of cerebral palsy characterised by abnormal, involuntary movement which, in my case, allows me only limited use of one hand.

I have never really been able to speak - just a few syllables before I was two ('mum', 'car'), but nothing after that. I have never been able to pick up a pen or a pencil. Yet words are my life, my passion. Words, especially written words, have become my bridge to the rest of the world.

As a child, I boarded at Harold Crawford House, the centre for Queensland's Spastic Welfare League in Brisbane, and attended New Farm State School for Spastic Children. I was homesick, of course, but twice a week Mum and Dad wrote letters to me ... letters rich with details of the life and home I had left behind in Bowen, Queensland, where I had spent my first five years. Those letters told me what mischief my brothers were up to, what Gran was doing, what the neighbours said, and even how the ocean looked. Wonderful words that made me feel as if I had actually been with them as they took part in these day-to-day activities. These were the first important written words I encountered and still treasure.

When I was six, my brother David was born, and my parents made one of their visits to introduce him to me. Mum, the baby and my other brother were outside, but one of the nurses, with a conspiratorial grin, beckoned to Dad to follow her. She pushed

---

1   Rynn, J. with Corrigan, J. (2013) *You Only Want Me for my Mind and Other Bedtime Stories.* Glass House Books, Brisbane.

me up to my desk in the classroom and positioned the electric typewriter, which had been fitted with a large keying plate to guide my fingers, right in front of me. Dad looked at me, then at the nurse, and smiled benignly. He so obviously was not expecting me to do much more than punch a few random keys and was already starting to make 'I'm proud of you' noises before I had done anything.

I was tense: so tense, my athetoid spasms cut in. But then, drawing on all of my determination and with an enormous effort, I pushed against the imprisoning spasm and my hand smashed onto the keyboard. Dad leant down, his head close to my hand, and looked up at me.

Slowly and cautiously, I punched down on the first key, then a second and then a third. Then I sat upright, pleased and proud. Dad's mouth dropped open and then shut – and then dropped open once more, without releasing a single sound. Before his eyes, the letters 'd' 'a' 'd' had been spelt out on the blank sheet of paper. It was the first time that his spastic son had communicated directly with him. We sat there in silence, our eyes gazing at the paper, then turning to stare into each other's eyes, and then looking back at that simple but profound word for a long time.

A powerful and unstoppable feeling rose up inside me. I could write words that were entirely my work. No one could stop me or take the sense of independence and triumph from me.

Cerebral palsy is no joke. As I say in my book, it is a ringside ticket to a lifetime of watching yourself deteriorate. But sometimes there are compensations.

For instance, when I was about nine, I had to undergo a gruelling operation on my brain which, although the athetoid spasms remained, gave me some more voluntary use of my left hand.

After ten days I had recovered and come back to school. I had no idea what was waiting for me. As usual, one of the nurses, Sister Nightingale, wheeled me to my desk where a large, familiar shape sat – the typewriter my teachers had provided for me, covered with its grey plastic cover. Nothing new here. But when I finally dragged off the cover, I couldn't believe my eyes. There was a brand-new electric typewriter, all elegant cream tones and jet-black keys with pearly white lettering. Who had done this? Was it my dad trying to find another way for me to express my feelings? Was it Mum thinking a beanie wouldn't be enough to console me for the pain and fear I had undergone during the operation?

Then Sister spoke from behind me. 'John, you were very brave to have a brain operation.' She put a hand on my shoulder and rubbed my back with the other one. 'You are a special, special boy. That is why I have given you a typewriter.'

I still couldn't believe it. I had been learning to use a typewriter for years, but that was strictly for school work. Here was a brand new one and it was mine. Mine!

I was made! Now I could write anything I wanted.

At the beginning of 1962, a new teacher arrived from England to take our class: Miss Pamela Hatch. She had jet-black hair, brown eyes full of the joy of life, and a warm, friendly manner. Most of all, she had a gift for teaching because she had the knack of getting on her students' wavelength. For the very first time, I understood how to work hard at school and at my typing. She loved that I typed notes to her, and, being the clever teacher she was, used this as a way of getting the most out of me. She asked me questions, such as what I did outside school, so she could get to know me better. One day, when I showed her my letters from Mum and Dad, I saw a glint in her eyes. The next thing I knew, I was using my typewriter to write letters back to my parents, all in my own words.

Now I was using words for real back and forth communication, I had a pathway out to the world. From their return letters, I could tell how pleased Mum and Dad were at getting letters from their non-verbal son ... letters creating his own accounts of his activities, thoughts, feelings, and ideas.

I couldn't stop. I wrote to Grandma, to my brothers, and many others. Everyone who received my letters was surprised and delighted. And wonder of wonders: I got letters back.

In addition to Miss Hatch, God has sent me many inspirational teachers. In 1966, He sent me Ms Curnow who would become one of the best of them all. She read to us from newspapers and books, and she did it in such a way that everything burst off the page and into the classroom. There I was, right where the story was set, hearing and seeing the characters, and taking part in all the adventures.

She also encouraged free writing, letting me type whatever I felt without the pressure of spelling correctly.

'John, let's get the words down,' she said. 'I don't care about your spelling because I can see your hand can't match the pace of your mind.'

Of course, my spelling had to be corrected afterwards, but she gave me the permission I needed to get my thoughts running across the paper as they came into my head.

Typing is hard, slow work for someone who can only use one finger of his left hand, and who pecks at the keys with the precision of an alcoholic woodpecker. If I needed to communicate and didn't have my typewriter, I just couldn't. To compensate, I evolved a series of facial expressions and noises that I still use to this day. These have always worked well enough if I am dealing with people who know me well but, in most cases, they're lost on people who are new to me. Ms Curnow took this dilemma on board and set about looking for a solution.

I could tell I was on her mind by the worried looks she gave me in class and the way she raised her finger as if about to say something only to walk away rapidly and talk to someone else. Then, one day, she asked for a meeting with me and my speech pathologist.

'Since you can type on your typewriter, John, why don't we get a board made up with the letters of the keyboard on it and a few simple words that you use a lot? That way, you won't have to spell them out all the time, and you can communicate back when people talk to you!'

It was brilliant.

During the next few weeks, I typed out what I wanted on my talking board, so a technician could get started on creating the layout. I loved writing and now saw a new dimension to the power and beauty of the written word. For the first time in my life, I could use words to talk with anyone, anytime.

And then there was poetry.

I was no longer a child. I was growing into a young man, and had all the feelings and emotions of any young man. I needed to express those feelings and emotions and I started to write poems.

Writing poetry was incredibly liberating and uplifting. I wrote and re-wrote, playing with ideas, words, images, emotions. As I got better at creating this form of art, I became more confident and more astonished at what I could do with words.

My speech therapist, Emily, was not much older than I was, and as a child had contracted polio. I marvelled at her strength and how she had used her ability to overcome adversity, complete a degree in one of the most difficult fields, and practise in such a demanding profession. But it seemed that having a disability helped her understand what others were going through, making her a much better practitioner. Emily let me talk about anything and everything, and in so doing, she opened my mind to many new ideas. She also read my poems.

One day she leant over my board, placed her elbows on my tray and her head in her hands. Leaning in really close, she murmured, 'You know, John, you could put out a book of your poems and let others enjoy your poetry.'

Why hadn't I thought of that? I just loved the idea, and when I suggested it to my teacher at school, he agreed, saying, 'John, that is absolutely brilliant!'

At fifteen, it was thrilling to 'have' writing, and to use it to start taking over the business of my life. I was not only going to be a grown-up, I was going to be an author. I had things to say. Writing is a gift from the great God Himself and I was not going to waste it.

So, for much of my fifteenth year, I worked furiously on my first book of poems. To my surprise and delight, I sold a hundred copies of that book. Publishing my own work and signing each copy gave me a special sense of ownership and excitement. But the most exciting thing of all was hearing back from enthusiastic readers who told me that they had enjoyed my poetry. It made me realise I had something I could give to the world.

In one of my poems, I say: *Hell had made a poet out of me.* That is true, but more than that, poetry allowed me to release the very deep feelings I could never express verbally. And poetry has done this better than anything else could have.

Whenever I have needed help, poetry has been there to help me.

I write a lot about freedom and how much it means to me, a person who fights every day to overcome restraints.

I write about love, and how girls only ever seemed to want me for my mind.

I write about the distance from family and the place of my birth, and how little things, like the smell of my mother's cooking or the sound of my brother's voice, were far more precious to me than they would be for most people my age.

Poetry empowers and enlivens me. By carefully arranging words on a page, I can affect another person's heart. What could be more powerful than that?

MIND OVER BODY

My mind is at war with my disabled body.
My mind has an idea.
My body takes a long time to do anything.
Then my mind gets mad with my body.
My mind tries to make my body do things quickly.
My mind should know my body cannot do anything quickly.
This war goes on and on.
It will stop when I die.

Since publishing my first book in the sixties, I have continued to write and self-publish, and have two books of poems and a collaboration to my name. My impairment, and the treatments I have undergone, have been hard, but they have made me an expert on my condition, which has led to other opportunities. For example, I have been asked to co-write and present papers in subjects ranging from assisted communication technology to PEG feeding and the loss of eating. I have become a motivational speaker and a disability advocate, enabling me to further other people's understanding and knowledge of what it is like to live and succeed with a disability.

Before speech devices were common, I would have to pester someone at conferences to read my work out loud to the audience. I was persistent, and never gave up until I got my work read ... no matter how badly.

It's always been like this: if I need to get something done, other people have to help me. For many years, I did my own typing, but now someone sits close to me while I point to words and they guess what I'm saying and key it in for me. Sometimes we do this for hours.

At one particular conference in Vancouver in 1996, my co-presenter, a speech therapist named Melanie McVie, suggested that I write a memoir.

It was a great idea, but I realised that, for a project of that size, I needed help. And that help arrived. But not immediately. It wasn't until 2005, nine years later, that my care facilitator announced that he had found me a new carer: John Corrigan. He didn't have much experience in caring, but he was a writer and was willing to help me with my memoir.

As it turned out, he was more than a writer: he was a good writer and became a good friend. He also learned how to be a good carer.

It took us seven years. I would point to a word, an idea, and he would try out different interpretations. Little by little, we'd reach agreement on what I wanted to say and how I wanted it told. Twenty-nine words a day and a lot of patience and perseverance. Little by little, I remembered past events and interactions – good and bad – and this reflection led me to a greater understanding and acceptance of my life.

We were always realistic about the future of the book. We reckoned we would self-publish and sell as many copies as we could ourselves, as that's what first-time authors can expect. So it was with the understanding that we would be paying the costs that we sent it to a publisher.

Then came their reply. Yes, they would publish, but it wouldn't be self-published. They would pay for the publishing because they thought there was a market for this type of book. Suddenly, we were real authors.

So, here I was, about to launch my book. Actually, there were two launches: one at radio station 4MBS with family and friends present, and another at a Cerebral Palsy League Picnic in the Park where support workers and those seeking support were able to experience first-hand what someone with cerebral palsy can do. Other people were able to see that those with cerebral palsy, and the organisations that support them, can achieve tangible, enduring outcomes. This is something I have always believed: that it is not in the thinking but the doing that we accomplish our goals.

Later, the entire book was read on radio 4RPH so that people with reading difficulties could share in it and be inspired. Then, by being available online, the book reached, beyond all expectations, a global audience, thus expanding the reach and impact of its message.

So what is its message?

That we all have abilities and disabilities. That we can all make a contribution to the world: some in big ways, some in smaller ways. That nothing we offer up is unimportant. That some of us have greater challenges than others, but we all need others to help us to achieve our ends.

My challenges have been considerable, but I have had a devoted family, and dedicated teachers. I have had sailing and fishing and art and poetry. I have experienced pain, but I have also known beauty. I have loved and been loved. And, I have been granted the power to express all of these things with words. Who could ask for more?

TWO

High-Viz Happiness
by Michael Kuhn and May-Kuan Lim

SMALL GARDENS WITH ROSES AND TIDY SHRUBS LINE THE DRIVEWAY THAT leads to Kathleen's retirement unit. I ring the doorbell and Kathleen welcomes me. When I compliment her on the heart-shaped wreath hanging on the door, she says that she's only just put up the decorations, a little late this year, because she's been so busy. I sit beside the Christmas tree while she settles into a lounge chair opposite. Then I say: tell me about Michael.

Kathleen: My husband, Reiner, and I brought Michael home from the hospital, a healthy baby. When Michael was just seven months old, Reiner died of cancer. Our daughters, Susan and Yvonne, were twenty-two and twenty-three at the time and they had already moved out. So for a very long time, it was just Michael and me.

When Reiner died, he didn't know that Michael was any different because by then Michael was sitting up like any normal child. I think I knew when Michael didn't crawl and didn't talk, but I pushed it out of my mind because I didn't want any more bad news.

As time went by, Michael got around by shuffling on his bottom, and made up his own sign language. For example, if he wanted a drink, he'd curl his fingers around an imaginary cup and lift it to his mouth. I knew if he was happy or sad, but he was hardly ever sad, so that made things easier for me.

One day, when Michael was about eighteen months old, I went to see the doctor and Michael was, of course, with me. The doctor said I should take him to the children's hospital.

At the children's hospital they told me that Michael had global developmental delay, and they booked him in for physiotherapy, occupational therapy, and speech therapy. It wasn't easy to keep all these appointments because Michael has a fear of doctors, dentists and needles. I can't understand his fear of needles, because he has a very high pain threshold and doesn't feel it. I know he doesn't, but it's something we've been working through all his life.

Michael started going to school at Gepps Cross Primary School, in a special class. He was just learning to speak then. They had a dentist who came to the school to check the children's teeth. Maybe it because the dentist's room smelt of antiseptic – I'm not sure – but Michael just would not go in. So the dentist had to go out into the schoolyard to see Michael. The dentist managed to get Michael to open his mouth, but Michael could not stand having rubber-gloved fingers inside his mouth. It's always been difficult, Michael with doctors and dentists.

By the time he was ten or eleven, he had moved to St Patrick's Special School. His teacher's husband was a dentist. Michael's teacher took Michael to her husband's dental surgery in North Adelaide, hoping to help Michael overcome his fear. The dentist managed to persuade Michael to step into his room. It was such a milestone that I took a photo of him sitting in the dentist chair. When we look at that photo of young Michael wearing sunglasses, I still say to him, 'You did well, Michael, look your mouth is open.' Because of the cost, Michael only went there once, but it was worth it because I use that photo to remind Michael of how good he'd been, and how he'd sat in the chair.

Since he left school, he's been going to see Dr Gryst in a special unit at the Royal Adelaide Hospital. Dr Gryst lets him take his time to sit in the chair. If he needs any work done to his teeth, he still has to be put to sleep. Michael's thirty-one now and his dentist is getting very tired.

It's not been easy. It's been slow. Everything's been slow.

―

When Michael was six, we visited his older sister and brother-in-law who were living in London. We were out shopping one day, and it was hot and very crowded on Oxford Street. Something must have caught Michael's attention because he dashed out – and disappeared.

Just like that, he was gone. I felt sick. Michael wasn't talking yet. He couldn't tell anyone his name, my name, his address or anything. I thought that I'd never see him again.

I went in to the jeweller's shop and they were very kind and allowed me to use their telephone to call the police. The police told me to stay put in the shop while they looked for him. I did as I was told, even though I didn't think they'd find him, and I wanted to be out looking for him. It was a sickening time for me, sitting there, helpless.

After about half an hour – even though it seemed like a lifetime – they'd found Michael and a police car came to get me. When I stepped into the police station, there was Michael, wearing a policeman's hat. I didn't know whether to weep or laugh. They had found him on top of a double-decker bus, confused and distraught.

The police asked me not to tell him off, because he'd been through enough. I was so happy to see him. There was no way I was going to tell him off, even though my daughter said, 'You should tell him off. You shouldn't let him dash off like that.' But I didn't let him anything – he just went!

It has been said that I am too soft on Michael. Reiner had a very strict and rigid upbringing, so he was the one who disciplined our daughters when they were growing up, but I am not like that.

My daughters tell me what I should do, but they don't have to do it. When you have Michael for thirty years, and not just for a few hours, you do what works. You do what you need to do to get some peace.

Perhaps it would have been different if Reiner had been with me while I was bringing up Michael. Perhaps it would have been easier. But I know that disabilities can cause conflict in families and many couples who have a child with disability split up over it. It causes conflict in the family; it shouldn't, but it does.

Because I was on my own, I did whatever worked. I used to take Michael out all the time just to get some peace because he always wanted to be doing things. He never played with toys, but was always making musical instruments, and loved going out to be with people.

Sometimes we'd get to the bus stop just as the bus was pulling away from the kerb. When he was a boy, Michael couldn't understand why the bus driver wouldn't wait for us. He'd get frustrated, and bang on the bus window and shout, 'How can you go off and leave us?'

It's embarrassing too. Michael used to have massive tantrums in public and because he looks sort of normal, people don't expect that behaviour. I'd feel awful because everybody was looking at me and thinking I should do something to control him, but they didn't know that when Michael gets frustrated, I can do nothing. He used to hold his breath when he was upset. Once, I had to run into a chemist to get help because he was turning blue.

So over the years, I've changed, and have had to swallow my pride.

I think it makes you stronger. I read in a carer's magazine that being a carer is like thinking you're going on a holiday to Bali but ending up in Holland instead. It's a completely different journey to the one you were expecting. You have to find your way through the health system, the education system, the disability system, and you do what you can to help your child, but it takes time, and it's a harder road than it is for a typical child.

~

At Michael's workplace, Orana (a disability support provider), I step up to the receptionist's desk and ask for Michael. I am ushered into a carpeted office. A man behind a desk stares at me, uncomprehending. 'Michael Kuhn,' I clarify. 'I'm here to visit Michael Kuhn.' Ah, the wrong Michael.

I am led instead to the back of the facility and given an orange high-visibility vest. I slip on the vest, then step through double-leaf doors into a huge warehouse. Electric cables hang from the shiny insulated ceiling high up, all the way down to machines on long tables arranged in two rows.

On both sides of the tables, people in high-vis vests are packing, checking and sealing plastic packets. As they work, they mumble, banter, grumble, and joke, so that there is an overlay of human voices above the whirl-whirl-whirl of a forklift shifting pallets in a far corner.

Michael is seated with his back to the doors. I pull up a plastic chair and sit beside him. The floor supervisor, Reuben, a big smiling man, calls out, 'Michael, my boy.' Reuben tips out a large cardboard box. Dried pigs' ears tumble out. The pigs' ears are translucent brown-yellow, laced with maroon blood vessels. They smell earthy, musty.

Reuben turns to me and says, 'You're writing about Michael? The good thing about Michael is that he is always happy.'

To Michael's right is Jane. Michael and Jane both have a line of masking tape on the table in front of them, with the numbers one to five written on it. I watch Michael placing five pigs' ears on the tape, three with tips pointing away, two with tips pointing towards him. Then he takes a flat orange plastic bag, opens up the wide base and puts three ears pointing up, and two ears pointing down into the bag. Sometimes he twists off circles of cartilage already punctured into the ears. Finally, he presses down on the self-seal plastic bag, stands it upright on a white plastic tray and reaches for another five ears and another bag.

As Michael and I work through the pile, Michael asks several times if I want to meet his friend, Fiona, who is sealing packages on the table opposite. Each time, I tell him that I will meet her when it's lunch. Michael asks how long till lunch. I look at the red and white Holden clock opposite and tell him how long more to wait. The plastic chair is starting to feel very hard and I notice the blue pillow on Michael's chair. Michael takes a swig from one of the two drink bottles in front of him. It is very hot and I wish I had a drink bottle too.

By this time, Michael has told me that every Thursday evening he plays basketball with Jane and her fiancé, who is working across the table from her. Jane must have heard her name mentioned because she turns her head very slowly to Michael and asks what he has said about her.

'I said you are my friend,' replies Michael. She nods, approving, then turns back to her work.

The Holden clock must be slow because when it finally gets to one o'clock, everybody continues working just as they have been for the past few hours. It's only when a familiar iPhone ringtone goes off, loudly – it must be through a speaker – that everybody stops and heads for the meal room. One by one, they retrieve lunches from a fossilised contraption labelled 'Employees fridge' and queue up to use the toaster. A notice stuck on the wall insists: 'ONE cup of coffee before work.'

Michael toasts his sandwich, Fiona's sandwich, and my sandwich. The three of us sit at a table. Most of the others sit in front of a large TV and watch the cricket. Michael gets up and returns with two glasses, small bubbles fizzing in the liquid, a can of soft drink shared with Fiona. Fiona is quiet but when I ask, she tells me how many brothers and sisters she has and how she is in foster care.

After lunch, I say goodbye, to Michael, Fiona, and other employees who have come to introduce themselves. Tomorrow, I will visit Michael's church.

≈

Rise Church is at the end of a quiet cul-de-sac, a two-storey building with a communications tower rising up to the sky. There is just enough remaining daylight for you to find your way to the main door. In the church foyer, fairy lights twinkle. Groups of young people are sitting on cushions, chatting. Others are queuing up at a small café servery.

I spot Michael easily because he is wearing a high-vis vest. As he turns around and sees me, his smile widens. He turns to a young man *next to him and introduces me as his friend. The young man, Frank, suggests that Michael show me around. Michael agrees. Michael really wants to get me a high-vis vest too but Frank tells him, twice: 'no need, just show her around'.*

Michael leads me into the main church auditorium. Portable white goal posts have transformed the hall into a soccer field. A soft ball hurtles through the air. The pulsating energy in the room follows its arc. It bounces off the low ceiling. Kids lunge. People cheer.

Michael joins in the chanting – 'go Joanne go'. Someone asks Michael why he is cheering for Joanne. Michael tilts his head for a moment and then replies that it's because she's a good youth leader. Why not cheer for Mark then? Mark is also a good youth leader. Michael considers this for a moment, then, with equal enthusiasm, he chants, 'go Mark go'.

On the large screen in the front of the auditorium shine the words: Welcome Home.

I stand with Michael, in a bubble of companionable silence. I get the sense that Michael is exactly where he wants to be right at this moment.

I turn to Michael and ask: why do you come here?

Michael: Because I feel happy. I feel happy at church. I am part of the security team with Pastor Rob. That's why I wear this vest. We make sure that the kids are safe and have a good time. After Youth, we have to make sure all the kids have left before we leave.

I wish Fiona[2] could come. Then she won't be so sad. Just stuck at home. Many of the pastors here are praying for Fiona. Pastor Rob is not here tonight, so if Fiona was here, I wouldn't be alone.

I had a birthday party here when I turned thirty. I went up on the stage in church like a worship leader. They put a Planet Shakers song

---

2   Not her real name.

on and gave me the microphone. I played the drums and the electric guitar.

Yvonne bought big blue balloons and she helped in the café. Her husband made masks and costumes and took photographs of everyone. I wore my black Planet Shakers T-shirt. Noel and Mark bought me a Planet Shakers cake. It was a good party.

~

Sunday morning. The chairs are back in orderly rows. The band is on stage and a young lady is singing. The congregation stands, sings, worships. During fast songs, Michael bops to the beat. During slow songs, Michael sways, slightly. His hands remain snug in his jeans' pockets. He smiles through every song. After the service, we have lunch with Michael and Pastor Rob at the church café. I ask Pastor Rob: how did Michael become part of the Youth security team on Friday nights?

Pastor Rob: Michael used to be part of the Youth Group. He has always loved being with young people. He also loves helping. When he became an adult, being part of the security team was a way for him to continue to connect with young people.

Every Friday, we have about 150 kids aged from ten to eighteen. Youth leaders run a separate program for primary school kids and high school kids. Having older people like me and Michael around, very visible in the car park from the time they drop their kids off, gives parents assurance that their kids will be safe.

With so many kids, we also have to balance the needs of the individual against the safety of the group. Once we had a kid who had head injuries and couldn't control his emotions, so we had to step in if we felt any of the other kids were in danger. In an emergency, I wouldn't expect Michael to take charge, but he can follow instructions and is a valued member of the security team.

Michael has limitations, but so does everyone. Sometimes Michael doesn't have the confidence to do certain things, but if I know he can do it, I will say, 'Yes Michael. You can do this.' I won't do for him what I know he can do for himself. I don't treat Michael any differently from other young people I work with. That's just how I roll.

Because Fridays are very busy, I often haven't had dinner before Youth, so Michael and I and the guys go out to Hungry Jack's afterward, and I think Michael looks forward to it. Don't you, Mikey?

≈

Kathleen has told Michael's carers that I will be visiting him at home. A van with a website address lighthouse.com.au parked in the carport assures me that I am at the right house. I notice an old-fashioned air-conditioner poking out of the old brickwork. It is a single-storey detached house, probably built in the 70s or 80s, with a nondescript garden, a few trees.

Michael opens the door for me. The corridor has bedrooms off to the right and I step in to the lounge and dining room to the left. Kathleen is sitting on the sofa. A big Christmas tree with tinsel and decorations are in the far corner, next to a door that says, 'Staff Only. Keep Locked.'

Michael introduces me to his carers (who work on rotating shifts) and his two housemates. On the wall hang framed photographs of Michael and his friends participating in a charity run, in a Hallowe'en dress-up. Michael shows me his room, painted blue, curtains closed, nightlight on, and two signs tacked on the walls. The store-bought printed sign reads, 'Life is a gift', while the other hand-written one advises, 'Keep calm, talk to staff, listen to music'.

Kathleen had told me that she was terribly depressed when Michael first moved out of home, so when I was alone with her, I asked: why did Michael move out?

Kathleen: A few years ago, I wasn't coping – I was worn out, overwhelmed, worried about Michael's future. Then I had a heart attack. It made me realise that I had to make sure Michael was settled somewhere before I passed on.

At the time, Michael was working in Coles two days a week, stacking shelves. He had worked there since finishing school. Coles takes quite a few people with disabilities. It was only two days a week, but they paid well.

After my heart attack, a volunteer said, 'You need him to work full time so you get a break.'

And while I was recuperating in hospital from a triple heart bypass, Disability SA started to try to sort it all out. Michael started working at Orana, where he could work every day of the week. About a year after I came out from hospital, Michael moved out of our home and went to stay in an apartment with another boy, a really nice boy, just the two of them.

I was really depressed when Michael left home. For over twenty-five years, it had always been just Michael and me. When he left, the house was so quiet, I could hear the clock ticking.

One night, Michael and the other boy had a fight. The other boy rang me because his parents were away. When they came back, they took their son away, because they were frightened. When the other boy moved out, I thought Michael would want to move back with me, because he hadn't wanted to go in the first place.

But he wanted to stay there, which shocked everybody. He stayed there and he started going out all the time. He went to town. He went to the beach. He went to the football club, talking to all the people. He loved the freedom. He just went where he wanted, and ate what he wanted, mostly a lot of junk food. His diabetes got worse, and he had to have laser treatment for his eyes.

He was very happy living alone, but it wasn't really working out. He was happy because he could go out all the time, and just go up to people. Once he knows you, that's it; Michael has a gift for making friends. I wouldn't do that. I would have to think about it before talking to a stranger. So sometimes I think it is not a disability, it's just different, you know?

And he's generous. When he sees the Christmas tree at K-mart, he wants to buy something to put under it. He wants to give to everything, you know? Which is another thing that is hard –he doesn't know money. He might go into K-mart with $5 thinking he can buy a TV. He's got a lot of challenges – money, language, writing – so I was surprised how well he did when he was on his own.

He managed better than I thought he would but he got into situations where he couldn't get himself home. Once he took the train to Noarlunga and lost his shoes at the beach, and I drove there in the middle of the night to pick him up. He would like to do everything, but he can't. It must be hard, to have your life so controlled: money, food, how he spends his time, where he can go. I mean we would kick up too, I reckon.

When being on his own wasn't working out for Michael, a very kind lady at Disability SA helped me find him this new place. Everyone in the house has different needs, and I don't really know how they make it work. It's not easy. There are some carers who really care, and unfortunately there are others for whom it's just a job.

Now, when Michael comes to stay for a week, I'm really glad when he goes back to his home because he's full on.

I know God is looking after Michael because of all the good people who have come our way, and because the ones who were not so good have gone.

~

When I think of Michael, I marvel at his obvious enjoyment of so many things: listening to music, working at Orana, worshipping at church. Then I think of the challenges he faces because of his intellectual disability: restrictions on where he lives, whom he lives with, where he goes. To get to know Michael is to witness a spirit of joy that rises above these challenges and is unbroken by these frustrations. I find that Michael brightens the atmosphere of a room he enters and cheers the people he meets. What a privilege it has been to have Michael call me friend.

THREE

Alice's Journey

by Alice Waterman and Emily Woolford

On 15 October 1993, I was born—a healthy young daughter—in the Mater hospital. My parents called me a 'pleasure' in their lives, remarking on my well-behaved nature and the beautiful thick, black hair that draped my head. Often a mischievous and fearless child, I walked and crawled much earlier than any of my siblings, showing a zest for whatever life experiences lay ahead. For example, while on holiday to Daydream Island, when I was not yet a year old, I saw a large resort pool and jumped straight in. Luckily my watchful father was there to catch me—as he would be throughout my life.

On Mother's Day 1994, I was infected by the sickness that paralysed me. My parents perceived it as a typical day, dropping their daughter off at child care. However, they were blissfully ignorant of the unanticipated impact this sudden illness would have on their healthy eighteen-month-old's life.

Called Enterovirus 71, it was an exceptionally rare and vicious illness that I had contracted from somebody who was already infected. This disease travelled into my infant digestive system and multiplied. While only causing a mild reaction in adult bodies that can deal with its effects, in little children the virus caused severe symptoms. I suffered from meningitis, which caused inflammation of the brain and spinal cord, due to the infection.

After infection, my condition rapidly deteriorated, and I developed a high temperature. Months later, I lapsed into a coma and was quickly rushed to the Prince of Wales Hospital in Sydney where I remained in a critical condition for several weeks, my tiny body fighting for life through sheer strength and determination. This was a distressing time for my family. The medical staff were unaware of what my condition was and could only keep me comfortable. Finally, I came out of the coma. However, I had to remain on ventilation and had become quadriplegic. It was a challenging time for my family; day after day they waited by my hospital bed, murmuring to me, with the unwavering hope of a response from their young daughter. My father's worries were somewhat relieved when he was able to secure half-days off work for the initial months I was in the hospital so he could visit me every day.

Several months after my eventual recovery, my family managed to ease me into a wheelchair so I could go outside for walks. My dad, Nick, even managed to get me into the car, so that I could return to the family home for brief visits. Even though I couldn't live at home, the challenge of growing up in hospital beds was eased by the constant support of nurses who brought a sense of comfort to the otherwise hostile environment. I was greeted daily by hospital staff, who always made me feel welcome.

After a period of time at the Prince of Wales Hospital, I was moved to the Royal North Shore Hospital. Thankfully this was located close to my family, which made hospital visits a lot easier. In 1998, my family returned to my parents' hometown of Adelaide, and I was admitted to the Women's and Children's Hospital.

I made lots of friends there with similar illnesses. We would play games and have dance parties—I look back on it with fond memories of my time there. I remember that the nurses, as a treat, used to take me for weekend walks around parks adjacent to the hospital, where they would read and sing to me. I loved these walks, the fresh air was a welcome relief from the hospital, and I enjoyed spending time with the nurses—many of whom are still my friends today. One day, one of the nurses on my ward even brought her puppy in; we were all excited because it was so friendly and cute.

After being at the Women's and Children's Hospital for several years, my parents eventually negotiated for me to live at home for four days a week and in respite care for three. I was thrilled at this prospect as it meant I could start at Trinity Gardens Primary School and socialise with lots of other children my age. I vividly recall my first day of school; I was terrified, as I knew no one except the nurse and support officers assisting me to adjust to the classroom environment. However, this all changed after I met my friends Bridget and Caela who befriended me instantly as I walked into the classroom. My teacher was also fantastic, and I still see her sometimes.

During my time in my various hospitals, I underwent a number of operations to make my life a bit easier. My first was a spinal fusion to straighten my spine, which had failed to develop healthily and was causing scoliosis. Only being nine at the time, it was a scary and challenging experience. But, the fantastic support network at the hospital kept me as comfortable as possible at all times. My family was also enormously influential in keeping me calm and happy before and after surgeries. It was only another three years before my next major surgery when I was age twelve. Skin grafts from my limbs were used to fill a hole that was allowing food to filter through into my lungs, leading to infections. The laryngectomy finally allowed me to eat and drink without fear of infection. My third and final operation was to straighten my foot to make mobility easier, so I could become more independent. All of these operations came with a vast amount of pain; however, it was well worth the initial suffering, and I am incredibly grateful to the hospital staff who have allowed me to enjoy life to the fullest capacity possible.

Primary school was filled with many fond memories. I particularly remember when I was granted my wish from the 'Make-A-Wish' charity. My all-time favourite TV show of the era was *The Saddle Club,* a feel-good drama about horse riding—one of my many pre-teen obsessions. Thus, when the charity got in touch and offered me an opportunity to meet the girls from the show, I couldn't contain my excitement—finally I could see and hang out with *The Saddle Club* in real life! These warm memories filled my childhood with joy. I was extremely fortunate to see some of my idols in person and see how beautiful and lovely they were off-camera.

My family initially found it hard to come to grips with the weight of my condition. Emma, my older sister, was only five at the time when I fell sick. She found it hard having a younger sister who had a great deal of attention from the rest of the family. My mother, Anna, would always make sure all my needs and wants were catered to as the loving parent she was. Eventually, Emma grew to understand my condition and matured to a mindset where she would help our family (and me) through thick and thin. My illness has banded our family together with a mentality of mutual support and helping each other out. In particular, my two younger brothers, George and Charlie, have grown up with a respect for all, and expressly those who encounter hardship because of a disability. They say I am an inspiration on account of my ever-optimistic attitude and my gregarious ability to connect with people. I am appreciative of how my siblings have got on with life and haven't treated me differently from any other person just because of my disability. They have also been paramount in helping me enjoy life and my childhood by getting me involved in social activities throughout my whole life. I could not have asked for a better family that supports me no matter the difficulties we may face.

In spite of my disability, I have been able to achieve many things that I am proud of to this day. I am particularly proud of my educational achievements such as graduating from Unley High School. Unley was a whirlwind of fun and hard work combined. Every day I was picked up and dropped home by our trusty taxi driver, Ray, who ensured I always had a safe commute to school. Similarly, many nurses and SSOs (support workers) supported my high school experience, assuring me that I could do things—even when I doubted I could. Continuing on to tertiary education after high school, I attended TAFE, where I completed two courses: one in women's studies and the other in education and skills development. These accomplishments have allowed me to prove to myself and others that a disability doesn't define your limits, and with hard work, you can achieve what you set your goals towards.

Nowadays I live in a house in Adelaide supported by SACARE and enjoy occupying my time doing things such as writing a blog named *Alice's Adventures*. I sincerely enjoy these activities as they allow me to write and give my opinion about many different areas. In 2013, the year I finished high school, I gained employment at Blend Creative, a computer graphical design company that hires many workers with disabilities. Working there gives me welcomed challenges such as learning how to use certain computer programs to create new and exciting designs for clients.

Looking towards the future, I am excited to move back home to Sydney to live independently in my own house. I would also like to find myself somebody to marry and spend my life with; having a partner to support and care for is one of my happiest goals. Another challenge is to be able to travel the world touring with a partner to share these experiences. Owning a pet companion to pat and care for in my new house is an ultimate ambition. I have enjoyed the happiness and comfort that dogs have brought me through my good times and challenging areas throughout my life. As such, in the future, I would love to have a pet to provide this companionship in the future.

Despite the complications of my disability, I've never failed to live life to the fullest, and I treasure the beauty the world has offered me. Not only have I overcome my disability, but I've also learned to love and embrace it, knowing that without it, I wouldn't be me. While I'm proud of my achievements, many of them would not be possible without the steadfast love and support of all the people who have helped me along the way. In particular, my family are to thank for my vibrant quality of life. Having a loved one by my side in both harsh and happy times has always been an immeasurable blessing. Life can often change in a split second, as it did when I first fell ill, and many believe that new circumstances will dictate your happiness and situations. However, what I have learnt from my illness is that you should not let circumstance shape the person you are or want to be. Instead, the people you meet, the lessons you learn, and the experiences you have will always dictate who you are and what you value. As I always have, live life with a smile, an open mind and, most importantly, an open heart.

FOUR

Struggling with Faith
by John Duthie

IF IT WERE POSSIBLE TO GRAPH MY LEVEL OF FAITH, IT WOULD resemble a sine wave that varied from top to bottom over a period. I realised the graph didn't represent a level of faith in God; it was my level of faith in the church, the leaders and followers of Christ. In turn, this affected my church attendance, service and my faith. It shouldn't be this way.

At the time of my accident, 11 September 2009, my levels of faith were low, as I experienced a church where people struggled with the power that comes with the position of leading a church. My children, Jasmine and Ben, were participating in a sports day at their school, as I headed over to my father, Alexander. A young student was chasing down a soccer ball, pushed along by the wind. I moved to pick up the ball. Although I did not see it, a tree fell on my head and back.

It happens. (You know what I mean)

The tree was a *Eucalyptus Sideroxylon,* known as an ironbark gumtree. One of the branches landed on my right side, hitting my head and my back, pinning me to the ground. I was fortunate to have teachers and parents with training in first aid nearby. The immediate problem was the loss of blood from the long split in my head, and towels stemmed the blood flow. The second issue was the broken leg and ankle, which were put back into place by a parent who was a nurse employed in the orthopaedics ward at the Royal Adelaide Hospital.

The first two to three weeks were just a hazy blur of time. I had 'anterograde amnesia', whereby I lost my ability to create new memories after the tree hit me, yet retained old memories. Following the accident, a representative from the school had mentioned to the media:

> *The children have all gone home and we've got the situation under control.*

I wish my health had had the same status. My spine was severed at chest level, and I had a concussion, a laceration to the head, broken collarbone, cracked ribs, damaged sternum, broken leg and ankle, a neck fracture, and bruising to the face. This most significant problem was a bruised heart, and the doctors didn't expect me to survive.

I spent thirty days in intensive care. I slept for most of the days. I required assisted ventilation for weeks due to the injuries to my chest. No wonder there was bruising to my heart. I remember suggesting to a doctor about the amputation of my legs, as they were of no use to me. I didn't want friends to be looking at my bashed body.

When a tsunami hit Samoa on 29 September, I wondered why God would allow this to happen; and why did He permit a tree hit me? Preventing a disaster or accident should be easy for an omnipotent, omnipresent and omniscient being. If He created the world within six days, then stopping a tree from falling on me should be simple. God was boasting in Jeremiah 32:27 of his abilities to do anything:

I am the Lord, the God of all mankind. Is anything too hard for me?[3]

The instant newsfeed of disasters and suffering around the world and the lack of miracles today as compared to those recorded in the Bible must be turning believers into non-believers.

I had doubts about supernatural theism. I had no problems with the 'theism' part, as I believed there was one God. My problem was with the 'supernatural' part, where God comes into the world when He feels like it from the heavens above, to perform supernatural miracles. I also struggled with the concept of prayer, which was the catalyst for the supernatural miracles. The cycle of prayer appeared to be: pray for something specific; when nothing changes, pray for something more general; when nothing changes, say it is God's will and pray for understanding; and most of the time the knowledge doesn't come.

I was questioning the little bit of faith I had left.

When I arrived at Hampstead Rehabilitation Hospital and immediately received my first wheelchair, I pushed myself to the internet kiosk and set a goal of writing a book about my experiences following the accident. It would cover the accident, ICU, spinal unit, rehabilitation and my return home, and be around 150 pages.

---

3   Holy Bible, New International Version®, NIV® Copyright ©1973, 1978, 1984, 2011 by Biblica, Inc.®

Around this time, I read the *Book of Job*. It is a poem about a man adjusting to his disability, and I was a modern version of Job. It was an appropriate place to start my journey of discovery about God and disability. Job was a person who worked hard, behaved well, obeyed God and tried to turn away from evil. He had children, and due to his efforts and investments, led a comfortable life. Satan challenged God, as the evil one thought Job only believed in God because everything had turned out well in his life. God gave Satan permission to test Job, and Satan took his wealth, but Job refused to renounce his faith in God. Satan stuck Job down with sores from head to foot. Job had had enough of the suffering, and complained in great detail including, 'I loathe my life'. He continued to protest and wondered where God was. Later God gave Job back twice as much as he had before.

I felt as if God had been protecting me and now the protection was removed. I was angry with God, and unlike Job, I wasn't given back twice as much from God. Biblical authors tell of a mighty and loving God, who is everywhere and cares for us, and who can control physical events such as winds and waves. I was asking God questions such as:

Why didn't You either prevent that tree from falling or make it fall somewhere else? That should be simple for a deity who created the universe in six days. Give me an answer, God! There are also plenty of miracles in the Bible, so how about making me walk again?

I tried praying for my situation and thought that there would be a miraculous cure on the anniversary of my accident. But 11 September 2010 arrived, and there was no miracle. My conclusion: 'Okay, goodbye God.'

One Saturday morning in October 2010, I awoke from my sleep. Usually, it would take some time to wake up. This time, I was only aware of one thing... pain. I started shouting out:

'Help me, I need help, I am dying!'

After a hundred questions and multiple examinations by many physicians, the cause of the pain was unknown. The pain was never-ending, and it continued past the weekend.

It has never ceased. The doctors placed me on a daily dose of 120 mg of MS Contin, a morphine-based pain relief. My dosage is the same amount as given to patients who are dying from cancer to increase their quality of life before death. A few months later, they discharged me. It was good to go home, but due to the pain, I didn't feel ready for this step.

I continued my study of God and disability, and unfortunately, Google sent me to Leviticus 21:17-23. I was shocked at the content, which I paraphrase as:

Anyone with a disability is NOT to come into the temple and offer food offerings to the Lord, as it will desecrate the temple.

A clear case of discrimination, and I should report God to the Human Rights Commission. Instead, I kept reading the Bible, hoping and praying it would get better. John 9:1-9 speaks about disability, and Jesus was asked whether a blind man or his parents had sinned. Before Christ, when people were born with disabilities, the belief was that the affliction was a result of the sin of the parents. 'Neither' replied Jesus, and He healed the man. God's glory came as a result of what happened after the accident, and there were no 'God-ordained' disabilities. Good can come out of bad.

I came across passages relating to disability, which improved my faith, as those with afflictions were loved and cared for by God.

Leviticus 19:14: Do not curse the deaf or put a stumbling block in front of the blind, but fear your God. I am the Lord.

Matthew 12:22: Then they brought him a demon-possessed man who was blind and mute, and Jesus healed him so that he could both talk and see.

Matthew 15:31: The people were amazed when they saw the mute speaking, the crippled made well, the lame walking and the blind seeing. And they praised the God of Israel.[4]

There were over thirty individual healings and twenty references to mass- healings in the New Testament. The majority of those healed had physical disabilities, such as blindness or paralysis. I wasn't aware of an SCI (spinal cord injury) healing in Australia and questioned whether these miracles occurred today.

I knew that Hebrews 13:8 says:

Jesus Christ is the same yesterday and today and forever.[5]

I Googled 'Australian Healing Ministries'. They would know about SCI healings in Australia, and I contacted the first ten ministries listed. They included John Mellor Ministries, Ellel Ministries, Healing Life Ministries, Katherine Ruonala Ministries, Victorious Ministry through Christ, the Order of St Luke the Physician in Australia, THE REVIVAL International Gospel Healing Ministry, Kenneth Copeland Ministries Australia, Dominion Grace Australia and Brisbane Healing Rooms.

The website marketing material included listings by: 'Healings and Miracles in Jesus' Name', 'Heal the Sick', 'Many experiencing instant healing in her meetings', and 'You can receive your healing'. A few weeks passed without replies, apart from the generic:

---

4   Holy Bible, New International Version®, NIV® Copyright ©1973, 1978, 1984, 2011 by Biblica, Inc.®

5   Holy Bible, New International Version®, NIV® Copyright ©1973, 1978, 1984, 2011 by Biblica, Inc.®

Thank you for your email. We are praying for you.

I reminded the ten healing ministries of my request, and gradually a few replies were received.

We don't keep records of God's healings in our ministry, so, unfortunately, we can't help you. Praise God for your healing.

What a cop out! I replied ...

A lame person that was walking would be remembered by your group. Why isn't it happening now? Your gift from God is healing. Or is it?

I felt sorry for people with SCI who respond to their claims of healing. Another reply included:

We appreciate your desire for fellowship. However, because our mailing list is confidential, we are unable to provide the information you requested.

Why couldn't they honestly respond with a 'no'?

Another ministry mentioned that no one with an SCI had been healed as yet. I gave them credit for reading my request and being honest. Katherine Ruonala Ministries gave the best reply, and I talked to a genuine and compassionate man for over an hour. He shared many miracles he was involved with, but no SCI miracle.

I was disgusted that six of the ten 'healing services' failed to reply to my email. Could it be they didn't want someone in a wheelchair to use their services? Instead, they would sooner claim miracles which cannot receive confirmation as being miraculous, and ignore 'harder' cases. I continued to pray, not knowing whether it mattered, and was open to God performing miracles, although my attempt to find proof failed. Was I trying to replace faith with evidence, rather than relying on faith?

I read over twenty books about people who either acquired or were born with a disability. Most were uneventful as they followed a path of describing the disability, medical treatments, and living with their supportive partner for the rest of their lives. After returning home to my family, I experienced confusion, hurt, disappointment, depression and stress. I assumed my wife was embarrassed by me, and this was why my wife along with her friends and relatives kept their distance from me. I felt as if I was receiving punishment for supporting Jasmine and Ben on their sports day.

The 'great escape' occurred on Sunday 11 March 2012 as my wife walked around the house, informing us of her departure to live in another suburb. I showed little emotion and said nothing. A few days later there was an admission of another man in her life. I asked for a name and was informed that he hadn't given permission to share his identity. Within thirty seconds I had an answer, as I logged into our mobile account, and dialled an often-called number. I heard the voice of a nurse who provided care for me during rehabilitation. After I hung up the phone, I said: 'This nurse will lose his job'.

The actions of my wife and the nurse were hard to accept, and I had thoughts of ending my life. I didn't know if I could do this. I piled up forty pain relief capsules before me and stared at them for an hour. The front door opened and my wife walked in—her mouth dropped, and we had a game of 'Hungry Hungry Hippos'. But rather than each contestant gathering balls, we were collecting as many capsules as possible. I amassed a total of zero pills and was taken by ambulance to the secure mental ward at the hospital. I had images of my wife and the nurse together, and this caused the drenching of my shirt collar with tears. I slept little, and the next day I heard someone say to me, 'You do not belong here'.

I looked around, and no one was there, and I asked to speak to the psychiatrist. However, I didn't mention the voice to the psychiatrist, when I asked to go home. Surprisingly, the psychiatrist discharged me.

Another day, another mental low, and I aired my feelings on Facebook, where I managed to meet my FB friend, Madie; Madie was the wife of the nurse. We started a friendship, and now are partners! That could be one of the strangest wife-swaps in the history of the world.

I had to set aside my emotions and consider whether there had been a violation of the hospital's Code of Conduct by the nurse; this was difficult to achieve. I didn't want my motivations to driven by revenge. Preferably, I wanted my actions based on justice; to ensure the nurse was suitable to continue working with patients. I prayed to God and took various courses of action. The Code of Conduct indicated that 'over-involvement' of a nurse with a person in their care includes inappropriate relationships with the partner or family of a person in the nurse's care, and anything sexual was an extreme case. Previously, my wife advised me to talk to mental health professionals, and all of them encouraged me to report the nurse.

I felt it was the right action to take, however, I experienced much anger and the investigation continued for years.

Staying home alone and thinking about life always resulted in me feeling depressed about life, and change was required. I spent time getting out with both Madie, my friends, and by myself. The purchase of a powered chair gave me more freedom, as it was easier to get out and about, and I could recline the seat to reduce the pain in my back. Before the accident, I enjoyed riding bikes, and the next mobility purchase was a tricycle. My hands operated the steering, the direction, the braking and the changing of gears. People would stare as I cycled past them on the road and I felt good as I was showing the world that life could still be enjoyable with a disability. Spending more time driving around in my station wagon helped my family, as well as improving my confidence. However, there were limitations. It took me about twenty minutes to pull my manual chair apart and place in the passenger seat, and another twenty minutes to put the chair together at the destination. I wanted to reduce the time, as well as have the option of driving my powered chair around, so I purchased a VW Transporter. Modifications were made to add an under-floor lifter, docking station, a three-way driver's seat, and hand controls. Now I could independently drive and roll anywhere.

The Nursing and Midwifery Board of Australia delivered their judgment on 21July 2017.[6] The behaviour of the nurse was considered to be 'professional misconduct' which is substantially below the standard expected of a registered health practitioner. A specialist psychiatrist made a point of the power imbalance in the relationship between people receiving care and the nurse providing that care. It took me back to Year Eight at Marden High School in 1978. I'd reached puberty late and the other boys were taller than me. Two students took advantage of a power imbalance and bullied me. The *bullyingnoway* website gives a definition:

> Bullying is an ongoing misuse of power in relationships through repeated verbal, physical and/or social behaviour that causes physical and/or psychological harm. It can involve an individual or a group misusing their power over one or more persons. Bullying can happen in person or online, and it can be obvious (overt) or hidden (covert). Bullying of any form or for any reason can have long-term effects on those involved, including bystanders. Single

---

[6] https://www.nursingmidwiferyboard.gov.au/news/2017-08-06-improper.aspx eftab720© AHPRA 2010, accessed [Wednesday 10 July 2019].

incidents and conflict or fights between equals, whether in person or online, are not defined as bullying.[7]

The nurse was a bully. The tribunal handed down a penalty of two years' registration cancellation, rather than a suspension. They suggested he should not reapply for registration. Standing up to bullies improved my self-esteem.

> God, grant me the serenity to accept
> the things I cannot change,
> Courage to change the things I can,
> And wisdom to know the difference.

Reinhold Niebuhr wrote the serenity prayer. It helped me cope with life, and in particular, the behaviours of people after my accident. I couldn't control what they did, but I could control what I did.

Following my accident, I lay flat on my back for around seven weeks, and I assumed this would be the way I lived the rest of my life. No one told me otherwise. The day I was transferred to a shower bed and sat up and had a shower was a relief, and it gave me hope for the future. Hampstead rehab introduced me to swimming. Before the accident, I could only manage two laps. My record now stands at forty laps (one kilometre), and my goal is to swim the same distance as the longest Olympic race, which is sixty laps. Immersion Therapy is the invention of my friend Peter Wilson. I use this therapy to swim laps at the bottom of a pool. My underwater record stands at thirty-two laps (800 metres), with a current goal of forty (one kilometre). Typically, I fall asleep early in the evenings and sleep in the next morning, as the exercise leaves me physically and mentally exhausted.

---

7   https://bullyingnoway.gov.au/WhatIsBullying/DefinitionOfBullying eftab720© Australian Education Authorities / The State of Queensland 2018, accessed [Monday 15 May 2017].

From the time I pushed my first wheelchair, I was aware of the difficulties encountered by those using this mobility device. As I came across access problems, I contacted the businesses or local councils and asked for resolutions. I progressed to advocacy for others with disabilities and came in contact with the Dignity Party. This is a political party in South Australia that stands up for disadvantaged people in society, including those with disabilities. The party accepted my application to run as a candidate in the 2018 state election in the seat of Torrens. In 2014, the Dignity candidate received 0.4% of the vote. I wasn't expecting to win the seat and set a goal of 5%. After a long campaign, culminating with the help of friends on election day to hand out 'how to vote' cards, I managed to receive 5.9%.

Unfortunately, our parliament's upper house seat held by our leader, Kelly Vincent, was lost. My experience was enjoyable, and I got to meet many new people or families with disabilities.

Building a home that better catered for my needs was another goal. It would include a pool that I could use whenever I wanted a swim, without assistance. The house would be a place I could invite my friends to, as well as being a family home, and I hope it will be finished by Christmas 2019.

Another goal was to travel to locations around Australia, and I have done this with Madie, my children and friends. We've been to Melbourne, Sydney, Perth, Brisbane, Gold Coast, Darwin and Mt Gambier. There were times when travelling with a disability was difficult, but it was better than staying home.

My journey of being hit by a tree; receiving injuries; dealing with chronic pain; being betrayed by people close to me—all affected my level of faith. The combination of events and outcomes is unique to me, and I am writing my memoir: *Alive and not Kicking*.[8]

---

8   https://alive-and-not-kicking.com

Writing the book is providing an opportunity to look back, and hindsight is always good. I can see that God was present, no matter what was happening.

Even if miraculous physical healing does not occur in your life, that does not mean that God cannot work in astonishing ways in your life. I survived a falling tree, and I believe this to be a miracle of God. I wasn't expected to survive the damage to my heart, let alone cope with a life of permanent paralysis below chest level. At the time of the accident, tens of people trained in first aid assisted me. I experienced a feeling of calmness during my thirty days in intensive care and cried only when the medical staff were sharing the news about my paralysis. Before my accident, I was swimming barely two laps, and miraculously now I can swim forty laps, using only 15% of my body.

I believe that due to God's intervention the events that caused me grief in life, such as the departure of my wife, helped my independence. I had no choice but to take care of my morning routine including toileting, showering and dressing without help. God can miraculously send people to arrive at my home and prevented me swallowing forty fatal capsules. Even the wife-swap event is wondrous, as I ended up with a partner who accepts my physical limitations.

I was waiting for a miracle, such as walking, and this didn't happen, but I missed all the other wonders that occurred! I look forward to more miracles in the future and the people that God put in my path. These people have increased my memoir by 250 pages! The graph of my faith is constantly heading upwards, and I spend time praying even though I have little understanding of it. As for healing ministries, I avoid them!

Jeremiah 29:11: 'For I know the plans I have for you,' declares the Lord, 'plans to prosper you and not to harm you, plans to give you hope and a future.'

FIVE

Living in Adelaide As a Couple with Disability

by Faisal Rusdi and edited by Marie Doener

FAISAL RUSDI WAS BORN WITH CEREBRAL PALSY CAUSING MOTOR dysfunction mainly in his hands and legs. He has been happily married to Cucu Saidah for nine years and works as a certified mouth painter. Faisal and Cucu use wheelchairs for mobility so coming to stay in Australia for fifteen months was quite an adventure. Here is their story.

The journey to reach the dream began

After some difficulty getting a visa, I arrived in Australia ready to support my wife, Cucu, who had a scholarship to study public policy at Flinders University, South Australia. It was a terrifying time because my carer was not permitted to enter the country, so I had to be courageous. My career as a mouth painter allowed me to get a visa where I could participate in art projects and study accessibility in Australia. It was a privilege to live in Adelaide, one of the most liveable cities in the world.

During the day, Cucu went to her office to study, which left me free to work on my art. My first activity in Adelaide was to participate in a painting exhibition organised by Amnesty International in collaboration with ARTillery Adelaide. I was the only artist from Indonesia to join in this exhibition and my painting 'The Power of a Diverse World' won. Such success was a big surprise after just two months in Adelaide. When I was not painting, Adelaide needed to be explored. Surprisingly, there were many places to visit in my electric wheelchair since public transportation and public spaces are accessible. I kept track of all the great places so that I could share information with other wheelchair users and to get ideas about what could be possible when I got home.

In Adelaide, I enjoyed:

- Art collections in the Art Gallery of South Australia
- Beautiful sunsets in Glenelg
- Watching people fishing from jetties
- Romantic moments in the Botanic Gardens
- Reaching the beautiful Morialta waterfall
- Exploring the Adelaide Gaol
- Seeing Hallet Cove, which was beautiful, but too many flies
- Camping at Victor Harbor
- Walking across the bridge to Granite Island
- Celebrating my eighth anniversary on the cruise in Port Adelaide.
- Participating in the Disability Pride Parade
- Boxing Day in Rundle Mall
- Fireworks on New Year's Eve in Elder Park

- Shopping in supermarkets and the Central Markets

Meeting dignitaries was very exciting: Kelly Vincent the youngest woman to be elected to parliament in Australia, and Martin Haese, the Lord Mayor of the City of Adelaide. Such honours are amazing.

The longer we were in Australia, the more daring we became. This included one long trip to enjoy a *Coldplay* concert in Etihad Stadium, Victoria. The bus ride took twelve hours, and it was accessible for wheelchairs so why not take advantage of every opportunity? Such freedom is not available in my hometown where accessibility is limited.

Friday prayers were another important part of our lives, so we were pleased to find several places that were wheelchair friendly:

- the Oasis Center in Flinders University with the university's Muslim community
- the Adelaide City Mosque,
- Marion Mosque
- Prayers at Adelaide University and the South Australian University
- Islamic studies with Kajian Islam Adelaide (KIA) and Masyarakat Islam Indonesia Australia Selatan (MIAAS).

Sports and Leisure

Since arriving in Adelaide, finding sports and leisure activities for electric wheelchair users in Adelaide was an important focus. It is difficult to stay fit when you are sitting in a wheelchair all day. Two activities through the Disability Recreation and Sports South Australia (DRSSA) website caught my eye. Immersion Therapy by organisation Determined2 and Push and Power Sports. Curiosity and excitement encouraged me to try these novel activities.

At first, Immersion Therapy was challenging because there was nobody to transfer me into the swimming pool. The first step was okay. I had to change into swimming clothes, but my wife helped me with that. It was easy since there was a hoist in the changing room. But getting into the water was a more difficult problem. At first, the instructors didn't know how to transfer me from my wheelchair to the swimming pool chair and then into the pool. Determined2 staff tried hard to find a solution and to improve their services. Finally, an occupational therapist advised them on how to transfer me easily and safely while keeping me comfortable. For months, my wife and I enjoyed immersion therapy on Friday mornings. Being in the water allowed me to relax, slowly balancing my body in the water. Finally, I reached a level where I could stand up in the water. This is such a pleasurable activity. I have to bring this experience to Indonesia. Many people would benefit from such a simple activity. However, I need to remember the importance of providing accessible changing places in each swimming pool or toilet changing rooms on the beaches. Hoists would also improve the lives of people with disabilities and their carers.

I love football, so I felt excited to play at Push and Power Sports on Monday evenings. They taught me how to play different games such as balloon soccer, rugby, football and hockey. To protect my legs, they lent me a bull bar and installed it on my footrest whenever I played.

Even though the sports were fun, they remained a challenge for me because the venue was far away. The first time I went there was on a Monday in the late afternoon. I went directly from the English class and had to take two buses to get there. The ride home involved three buses which was very complicated.

My wife prepared bus routes and schedules on 'sticky notes' which I kept handy at all times. My first night was quite an adventure. Getting to the centre was fine even though it was an unfamiliar area, but I got stuck on the way home. It was dark, and there was nobody around when I left the facility. Where was the bus stop? Frustrated, I had to return to the gym, hoping to find some help. Jacob, the Development Officer, was about to lock the gate and leave. Luckily, he stopped what he was doing to help me. We finally found the unlit bus stop and waited together until the bus came. It took two hours to get home because the route took three buses. What a journey! I finally arrived home at 11 pm. I had never experienced such late-night travelling, but I loved these sports, so it was worth it. Travelling far and coming home late was a small price to pay.

Services for people with disabilities are good in Adelaide, and this promotes equality. There are many so different kinds of supports available for people with disabilities to allow them to enjoy life. On public transportation, there are options that people with disabilities can obtain based on an assessment result. I got a mobility pass to use on Adelaide Metro public transport. To obtain this pass, I had to go through my GP (doctor). Once I had the pass, I still had to pay A $70 per month. This allowed me unlimited trips with no need to validate my disability every time. This is a great service, but you have to travel many times to make the cost worth it.

Another support in Adelaide was a Companion Card. The card helped a lot because often I need a companion on long trips. Toileting during trips or special occasions is impossible for me without a support person. It is also nice for the companion because the activities are free for them as long as they accompany someone with a disability. We used the Companion Card when riding the Metro, watching movies in the cinema, attending concerts, and visiting museums and the zoo.

Unfortunately, many places are unreachable by Adelaide Metro public transportation, but there are more ways to travel around the city. A taxi seemed like it would be a good option for important events. Many people use the taxi voucher scheme that is available in Adelaide. Unfortunately, I was not eligible because this was only for Australian citizens or permanent residents. Wheelchair accessible taxis are available, yet they are very expensive.

Another problem with taxis is that the fees are unpredictable. There were many times we felt cheated. We had a very bad experience with a taxi in Melbourne. The driver asked us for a lifting fee of $25 for each of us, plus $26 for the fare as stated on the meter. These fees are not fair. In Hobart, a taxi driver asked $10 for lifting and made up the total amount of fare, it was $65 on the meter, but the driver asked us to pay $95. In many cases, the taxi drivers switch on the meter before we get onto the ramp and only switch it off after we were all finished out of the taxi. Of course, it adds additional dollars on the meter. I think lifting fees and wheelchair safety belts should be part of the service not as additional fees. These examples show how attitudes and services need to be improved. People with disabilities who are not Australian citizens need to be aware of these practices. Before you get in the taxi, you need to ask what the fees are and about how much the ride will cost. Don't negotiate a price and make sure the meter is not running until you start your journey. I shared this information about disability services with other international students with disabilities. I was glad to see some of them follow my advice and join in a variety of activities.

Most Australian people are kind, and their manners in the public spaces are impressive. Many people apologised for walking in front of my wife or me and gave us space to use the footpaths.

Wheelchair users get priority in public areas and on public transportation.

The Adelaide Metro bus drivers were good to us when we travelled by bus yet a few of them need to be better trained. Some of the bus drivers familiar with us were kind: smiling at us and greeting us with kindness. However, some bus drivers need to improve their attitudes.

Many people with cerebral palsy, like me, don't like sudden loud noises. So it is frustrating when drivers loudly slam the ramps down. In these cases, dust from the ground sprays up into my face. The only option is to stay further back from the bus kerb as the buses stop. The older model buses are worse. The ramp is located in the middle of the bus. In this case, the dust spreads to other passengers in the wheelchair seating area when the driver puts up the ramp. That is why I prefer buses with ramps near the front door.

Another frustration was when a passenger sat in the wheelchair space. They didn't fold up the chair as it was supposed to be. Sometimes I had to argue with passengers with a baby pram, or the driver, because they used the wheelchair space. I know it is law that wheelchair space must be vacated when required by the wheelchair passengers. I love babies, but a baby could be held by their parent/adult, and the pram could be folded. Our wheelchairs cannot fold up; we have to sit somewhere. Common sense and good manners would help make the bus ride comfortable for all people. Bus drivers should know and understand the rules of priority seating and remind passengers of the rules. It is not fair for the person in the wheelchair to be the only advocate in these circumstances.

Other problems occurred when travelling on a bus. Whenever I travelled without a companion, I always reminded the driver to stop at the destination I needed, but often they didn't remember or ignored it. I had to be paying attention at all times. Another problem occurred when three wheelchair users wanted to ride the same bus at the same time. There are only two spaces for wheelchairs. This causes inequality and takes away access. Imagine if there are three wheelchair users or more who want to go to school or a doctor's appointment. Of course, it is not possible to wait for the next bus because their appointment is at a set time. There should be at least three or more wheelchair spaces on each Metro bus. I will bring these ideas to Indonesia to advocate for better public transportation service.

Indonesian cultural ambassador in Adelaide

While I was in Adelaide, an amazing cultural event, the tenth *Indofest* 2017, was held honouring Kampung Indonesia. It was a big event to introduce the rich culture of Indonesia, specifically that of the five biggest islands. The event was held in Victoria Square, a strategic location in the city of Adelaide. I was proud to be the 'Walikota' (Mayor) of Kampung Indonesia. People were happy with my efforts on the organising committee, including the 'Kepala Desa' (Head of Village) and other committee members as we worked as a team. The event included workshops, traditional games for children and traditional foods to eat. As a disabled person in the event team, I tried to make the *Indofest* event accessible for all, so people with disabilities could enjoy the event. I had to make sure there was an accessible toilet and that the committee members and guards were trained, so they were able to assist people with disabilities. The festival needed to provide a place for people in wheelchairs to watch the show on stage. Although not yet fully accessible, I tried my best to do everything I could to make the event comfortable for people with disabilities.

I joined my wheelchair friends and introduced them to each stall which shared information about our culture. Also they learned about traditional musical instruments and clothes. They were very happy to experience my culture, and of course, increase their knowledge about Indonesia.

It was not an easy thing to organise the Kampung Indonesia. The biggest problem was a lack of assistance to accompany visitors with disabilities around the event to be sure each one had access. Many of the organising committee members were students who were busy with their studies, Indonesian-Australian citizens, or spouses of students. They were busy with their daily life, such as work, and didn't know much about accessibility. The volunteers needed training on how to work with people with disabilities. Also, time was limited for me, because at the same time, I was preparing solo painting exhibition for November.

Painting while in Adelaide and the solo exhibition
My Australian travel wish-list included having a solo exhibition in Adelaide. Yet, it was difficult to hold an exhibition within the disabled artist community in Adelaide. I contacted two different disabled artist organisations in Adelaide. They asked for pictures of my paintings which I submitted as required. However, there was no response from either of them. My perception was these organisations prioritised local or Australian artists first and did not have space for an Indonesian artist.

Another problem at this time was housing. For the first four months, we lived in campus accommodations, and in January 2017, we had to move. Each room cost $250 per week, and since we had to pay for two rooms, we were paying $500 per week. This was too expensive. There was no assistance or information from the International Student Services about where to find accessible accommodation in Adelaide. Eventually, we found off-campus accommodation located a bit further from Flinders University. It was not ideal for wheelchair access, but we could manage. The landlord was an artist who was very helpful.

After a few weeks of living in the new accommodation, I discussed my wish to have a solo painting exhibition with my landlord. He suggested the West Torrens Auditorium Gallery because they had accommodated him with an exhibition. I was quite open with him about needing a sponsor to cover the costs of venue, catalogue print, curator fee, publicity and everything else an exhibition would need. After few days, the landlord advised me that the West Torrens Auditorium Gallery would sponsor my exhibition for free. I was surprised about all those free items, and the exhibition was set for November. Then the realisation hit: I had less than four months for preparation of at least nineteen paintings. This was my dream, so I set to work at once.

Every day, from eight in the morning till six in the evening, painting was my life. There were only breaks for lunch or prayer. Weather was one of the challenges to my work on my paintings. It was winter, and it was cold. I paint by lying with my tummy on the floor. My elbows hold me up so that I can use my mouth to do the work. My teeth and lips hold the brush to make the painting. My wife helped me to prepare for work every day in the morning before she left for the office. With the limited time, I decided to paint in the Impressionist and Pointillism styles to speed the process and produce paintings using media oil on canvas.

Finally, I finished the paintings and held my solo exhibition from 13 November to 3 December 2017. In concurrence with my experience in Australia, the title of the exhibition was 'Colour of the Journey'. I showed twenty-one paintings of different places that I had experienced on my journey. Throughout the exhibition,

I wanted to introduce Indonesian culture such as food and traditional musical instruments. While I lived in Adelaide, some people were negative about Indonesia, so I wanted to change that attitude. The Indonesian Adelaide Association, IndoPeduli, provided free food and musical performances with traditional instruments for the event. The exhibition was a huge success. It was opened by Dave Gordge, Director of the South Australian Department of Foreign Affairs and Trade (DFAT) and the Hon. Kelly Vincent, MLC. Many people came to the launch, as well as, visitors during the three-week exhibition, and ten out of twenty-one paintings were sold. I was tremendously happy and felt the four months of hard work paid off.

Happy with Cucu's Graduation
Eventually my wife finished her studies on time. I was so proud of her especially on graduation day. The audience applauded when she crossed the stage and received the parchment from the Chancellor. It brought me to tears reminding me how hard we worked to get our dreams to come true in Adelaide. We overcame many challenges along the way as she got her master's degree on time and I did a solo painting exhibition. I remembered the times when we lived at Flinders University.

Often my wife stayed late on campus doing her assignments or finishing early in the morning. Sometimes I stayed alone at home, other times accompanied her on campus. We would wheel across the bridge from the main campus to the housing, up and down the hill in the middle of the night. Sometimes we didn't get to bed until 2 am. We rolled through the quiet paths and tall trees in the dark, even if it was cold and windy.

Sometimes I accompanied her until morning. We prepared small blankets and snacks for those all-night stays on campus.

We followed this kind of rhythm until we moved off campus. One day my wife stayed on campus until 3 am so I stayed with her and then we wanted to go home because we were tired. A wheelchair accessible taxi came to take us to our home on Anzac Highway. The call operator was surprised, and asked 'What are you doing there?' Maybe the call operator was curious about why these two persons in wheelchairs were still awake and on campus. But Cucu needed to finish her work, and we did what we had to do. Sometimes, we even stayed on campus the whole night and went directly to the Sunday market in Brighton. That was so tiring because I had to sit on my wheelchair for long hours. However, all the hard work had paid off. Years ago, Cucu's sibling said, 'It's better you finish your master's degree instead of marrying Faisal. He will be an obstacle for you!' But that was not true. We had supported each other, and our dreams finally came true.

We promised to continue our advocacy work on the rights of people with disabilities when we get home to Indonesia. Campaigning for accessibility for all and teaching the universal design concept is important. We experienced the freedom to go anywhere with public transportation even though we were both in wheelchairs. The public facilities were so accessible for wheelchair users that we could enjoy many places. All the memories of Adelaide are so special. I am going to miss all my Oz friends especially the Push and Power team members. I will miss playing balloon soccer, rugby, hockey and football with them because there are no such games for electric wheelchair users in Indonesia. I will miss all the instructors of Immersion therapy in Determined2 who were very kind and professional in providing services for people with disabilities, and those at the Adelaide Aquatic Centre as well. I will miss all the very kind English teachers in Ascott Community Uniting Church and Oasis at Flinders University. I will miss all the wheelchair access facilities, public transport which really supported my independence and freedom.

Now we are home again in Indonesia, we will use the information we gathered on our visit to Australia. Cucu learned about public policy and will apply her knowledge. She will try to find work that fits her passion for disability advocacy. I will also continue to advocate for accessibility in Indonesia based on my experience in Australia. My friends, family and the whole community can enjoy a better world when we provide access to everyone.

SIX

See the Real Me

by Jacy Arthur and Diana von der Borch-Garden

HAVING A BABY REALLY CHANGED ME—MY SON, LUKE DANIEL Arthur, was born 24 Nov 2000. 'Relax and the baby will relax with you' my mother and nana used to say. 'Don't worry so much and just enjoy.'

When we have a baby, we all look to our mothers for help and guidance, and so after Luke was born, I moved into Mum's house to make it easier for the baby and me. My dear nana stayed with us for the first two months of Luke's life. There's no way I could have done this on my own.

As a sole parents, we feel obliged to be perfect parents, and to make it easier for our children, we do our best to keep in contact with their fathers. There's always the worry though, that at any time, we may lose our children. For someone with a disability, that concern can be intense. I feared that my disability could be used against me, no matter how good a mother I was, nor how much I loved Luke.

Luke is an eighteen-year-old teenager now—and I'm learning to step back and let him grow, which is hard to do since teenagers are so lazy and careless at times. According to my mother, I was the same.

At his school I was worried that Luke would be teased because he had a 'wobbly' mum, so I kept my distance. As he grew older, especially during his high school years, I kept well away. I would make sure our parent/teacher meetings were during quiet times at school, or when there were hardly any kids around. It was a hard decision to make, especially as I was on my own. I remember how difficult it was for me with my spastic movements and I hated it, and so for the sake of my son and his dignity, I just had to let him have as normal a childhood as he could.

My son and I are very close, and as he gets older, our bond only grows stronger; I know we'll be best mates once he reaches adulthood.

Luke has always been a very likeable, popular kid at school—everyone loves him because of his good nature, his good manners and the fact that he's very funny. He will be in Year Twelve next year.

I mentioned earlier that I had no intention of Luke being teased for having a 'wobbly' mum but is true. I am wobbly.

I was born in Mildura in 1972, with breathing problems and not expected to live, and if I did, I was expected to be a vegetable. It must have been a very stressful time for my parents. Nevertheless, I defied the odds, got on with my life, faced many challenges, studied and gained employment as a graphic designer.

I have no idea which comes first. Are we born with the personalities that will help us meet challenges such as Cerebral

Palsy and a hearing impairment, or do we learn to be determined, patient and resilient because we have a disability? I know for certain that having good family supports certainly helps. Decent, strong-minded people around you, who encourage you from the start are essential.

Perhaps if I tell you a little about myself, we may discover which it is together.

During the first twelve months of my life, I went through hundreds of tests, and was finally diagnosed with Cerebral Palsy and later, they found out I also had a hearing impairment. For a lot of children with a hearing impairment, they can learn sign language, but for me, it was difficult, as I couldn't coordinate my hands sufficiently to communicate to others, so I learned to lip-read. As a teenager at school, lip-reading became a wonderful asset for me, because I was able to lip-read what the teachers were saying to one another, and then I would pass that on to my friends. You can imagine, how popular that made me. Privy to conversations hearing kids couldn't see. What fun!

When I was younger though, I often got words mixed up, for example, I would be told to put my thongs on, and I thought they were calling them 'thong thongs'. Another time, I remember asking for peanuts and tomato sauce for lunch. My mother was horrified at the combination of food I requested and said 'NO!' so I went over to the cupboard and got the tin out of the cupboard to show her. I thought baked beans were peanuts. They looked similar. I also gave things other names at times, such as half-moons for croissants, and kabanas for binoculars.

I was a bit of a daredevil according to my mother, whether that was using my walker as a baby or tearing around on my three-wheeler bike.-I never saw myself as different, and just accepted the way I was. My parents never treated me any differently than they did my sister, who was two years older than me, so I didn't suspect anything.

At the age of five, I remember seeing my mother sobbing. It had been decided that the best thing to help me progress was to fly down to Adelaide, six hundred kilometres from home, to board at Regency Park for twelve months. There I would learn some of the skills that would help me in life. So, there I was, this little girl aged five, flying by herself from Broken Hill to Adelaide and every three weeks or during the holidays, I would fly back to Broken Hill to be with my family. What a brave little girl I must have been, leaving my family behind, and facing all those new challenges on my own.

It was probably when I was about seven years of age that I realised I had a problem, as I could not tie my shoelaces or do up my buttons. (I still have the same difficulties) I've come to terms with the things that I can't do, and if I want to move forward, it's a matter of accepting those things or working out how to solve problems. I have to work out how I can ł do things in a different way and I always find a way.

At eight, I joined the Brownies, and I'm sure that what I learned came in handy for the adventures I sought later on. I was a determined child, and I suppose some may call it being stubborn, because I had no intention of asking for help. This attitude enabled me to be who I am today and to achieve the things I have, such as climbing Ayers Rock (Uluru); going on camps where the Landcruiser was bogged in mud for hours; travelling through the Goyder River with water up to the windows and travelling the rough tracks to Cape York.

There were times, though, when I started to think of myself as 'special', because whenever we went out, people would stare at me, and because I have a pleasant nature, I saw it in a positive way. That reality came crashing down years later when we visited an aunt and her partner who had a new movie camera. The thought of seeing ourselves on film was exciting at first, but to see how I walked, I thought, *surely, I'm not that bad?* I was very emotional and laughed with the others, but deep down I felt angry and depressed but just for a fleeting moment. It was a matter of getting over that initial feeling of shock. I had always seen myself as normal and had been treated as normal, and had normal friends and everyone was normal, that is, except me!

If you were to ask me if it's a good idea to treat people with a disability as 'normal', I would have to say 'yes'. There's something that feels right about being treated the same, a sense that even though you might be different, you can still achieve your goals. You might have to adapt the way you do things, but that's okay. You see, it's more about the process of doing something that helps me feel good about myself. My disability restricts me enough, so I don't want to feel restricted by what other people think I can or can't do. I want to be able to go out there and give it a try.

I believe the most important advice I could give parents of children with a disability would be for them to step back, and let their children learn new skills, and let them learn to find a way to achieve their goals, no matter how small they may seem. Support and guide them, but let them make mistakes, or feel frustrated, because, in the end, it helps them to feel good about themselves. Love them and care for them just the same as you would any child.

My family is my strength, and they have supported and guided me throughout my life and encouraged me to go out there and achieve my goals. They gave me the inner strength I needed to be successful in life.

There have been a couple of turning points in my life.

The first was when Luke was born. I began to focus on my son more than I focused on myself, and I no longer worried about strangers or people generally out in society, or their rude stares or comments. Changing my focus to something outside myself also changed my perception of the people I thought I knew.

I had a renewed sense of inner strength and had no hesitation in standing up for my son, because I wanted to make sure, that he would have the opportunities that I missed out on, when I was a child.

I wanted to make sure that Luke would have great childhood memories and have the opportunity to travel and go on holidays as I did with my family. I wanted my son to do well at school so I made sure he learnt as much as he could. Now, I also encourage him to keep in touch with his teachers.

One of the other decisive points in my life, was when I turned forty. It was then that I realised that I may never be accepted as 'normal', well at least as far as society was concerned, so I thought *stuff them!*

I can distinctly remember that moment, and thinking to myself, that I have achieved some amazing things in my life, by just being myself, and then and there, I decided not to worry about others any more. They have no idea who I am and what I've achieved, but I realised that I know who I am, and what I've achieved, and that's the most important thing. I realised I don't need their approval.

I remember thinking that those strangers may stare at me – you know those 'staring moments' – and then they will disappear and forget all about me and get on with their lives. There will always be strangers, and there may always be those 'staring moments,' but I've come to accept that, and I have come to accept that I cannot please everyone.

I've become myself more in public, eating with ease in cafés and restaurants, and yes, people will always stare at me, so I might as well make it interesting for them, and say hello with a smile. That's when the staring stops.

The young ones are usually busy these days on their smartphones, so I am not bothered by them anymore. In the end, it's about my perception of what they might be thinking about me, and that can change, depending on whether I'm having a good or a bad day.

So, this brings me back to the question as to whether we are born to cope with a disability or whether we learn to adapt to the disability. I was born with the spirit to challenge myself, whatever those challenges were, and to not let anything stop me, and I was born to an accepting and supportive family, who didn't restrict me from doing things because I had Cerebral Palsy and a hearing impairment. Like all successful people, I was encouraged to be who I could be, and to work towards my goals, and achieve them. As a mother, it is my goal to do the same for my son, who is my highest priority. The fact that I have a disability doesn't stop me from being a good mother, or to teach my son to be a decent person.

SEVEN

Do You Ever Feel Like You Just Don't Fit In?

by Phillippa Smoker

Do you ever feel like you just don't fit in? You feel isolated, and the fear of not belonging engulfs you? That was my life before being diagnosed as autistic at the ripe 'old' age of thirty-five. Being diagnosed was a life changer for me; it felt like all the parts of my life clicked together and began to make sense. I started to understand myself.

My childhood was a traumatic time with numerous foster care homes. The foster home I arrived at just before I turned eight is the most memorable. Peggy, whom I came to call Gran as she treated me like one of her own grandchildren, became my permanent foster home until I moved out at age seventeen.

For a time, life was very mixed up, and Gran told me I didn't know day from night and that I would scream for hours on end, yet I barely remember these times. With Gran's patience and perseverance and as well as therapy I slowly came forth from that dark hole that I had been living in. Even though I no longer felt the effects of the trauma I experienced, I still felt different; I couldn't put my finger on it.

At the age of twelve, during a court hearing, I decided on my own terms to no longer see my birth mother. The scars of my upbringing and the mental abuse that I suffered were too deep for us to mend our relationship, and I no longer saw her as my mother but as a stranger who wasn't connected to me. I still feel this way today. Throughout my time in foster care, I did see members of my biological family. Many of them live interstate, and we regularly keep in contact. The last time I spoke with my mother was via the telephone on my wedding day; she has since passed away.

Many of my autistic behaviours as a child were put down to trauma, and as an adult and looking back, I think I felt frustrated. I would do anything to try to fit in and therefore wore a 'mask' for most of my childhood. I struggled a great deal as a child and if I had been diagnosed then instead of as an adult I may have understood myself better. Trying to wear that mask all of the time was exhausting, and this may explain why I struggled more in adulthood

By the age of twelve, I was set in my ways. I enjoyed a love of reading and creative writing and much of my time was taken up with this. By being able to escape into those fantasy worlds, I was able to disappear from reality, even if only for a few hours. It became problematic for a time as it was all I would do and it captivated me in primary school, I did have friends, but I wasn't one to socialise outside of school. I wore my mask until I commenced new friendships in Grade Ten at high school. Then I could mostly be myself with them, and they would accept me for being me.

By the time I was a senior in high school, I was living in my flat in a large apartment block. I enjoyed having my space where I could do my own thing, but I did get lonely. Struggling with friendships made it hard for me to connect outside of school. A few months later, I was introduced, via friends to my husband. We have now been married for over seventeen years, and although we have had our ups and downs, he has been my rock ever since we met. He is a patient person who stuck by me since the beginning. I barely could say two words in the first two weeks of dating, and now we talk to each other a lot more as I feel comfortable in his presence. We have our own interests, and that helps our relationship to work. I couldn't ask for a better ever-present life partner or a better father to our children.

Around the same time I met my husband, I took in a tiny rescue male kitten. The little bundle of fur was riddled with fleas and needed a vigorous flea treatment to rid him of all the nasties. His coat was pure white, and his eyes were blue—not the watery kind of blue you see, but a deep ocean blue. Unlike many other pure white cats, he had no hearing loss as is prone in white cats. I called him Jasper, for no other reason that I liked the name.

Jasper became what I now define as a therapy cat. At the time I wouldn't have known what a therapy cat was, but I believe this is what he came to be for me. Jasper had the tolerance of a saint and was almost always by my side. He would purr at a single touch from me, and when he touched me with his claws, he always had a gentle touch. Jasper knew not to hurt us even amidst play and would grab at our feet as we walked past. He could be resting on an armchair and would hang out a paw as the kids walked past to grab onto their clothing which would make them jump and we would giggle with laughter.

Back in my late teens I worked in retail, and it was my first job out of school. It was something I could do because I could speak to a script without getting caught on the spot. Not knowing what to say is still is a big struggle. My workplace was an hour's bus ride away, and I caught the bus to and from work back when I could tolerate it.

Jasper would follow in my footsteps as he didn't want to be left behind. If permitted, he would have ridden the bus all the way to work, and I probably would have taken him with me! When I caught the bus back home, Jasper would be waiting for me again, and I could see him from the bus window as the bus pulled up to the stop. We would then walk home.

Even as he got older, when I walked to the shops with the kids, he would run after us, meowing as to ask where were we going and if he could he tag along. As he was getting old, I would have to shoo him home as I feared he would get hit by a car. At the time, I didn't understand how unsafe it was to be an outside cat, and our current cats all now stay inside unless I walk them on their leads.

Jasper had a fascination with water, and whenever I went to the bathroom, he would be waiting in the bathroom basin for me to turn on the tap so he could play with the water or to drink. He preferred fresh running water as compared to the water I placed daily in his bowl. He repeated this behaviour if I took a shower or bath. I have many photographs of him with his paws fully immersed in a water tub that we had outside for the birds. He was much more dog-like than a cat and was my ever-loyal companion for nineteen long years.

Even as he grew older, he was still able to rough and tumble with Katsuma (one of our other cats). In his older years, the kids had him playing with a piece of string! It was almost like he knew and had to have a play with them one last time.

I have never met another cat like him, and I have had other cats since him. I'm sure people hear that a lot, but he was special. Jasper was my sleeping buddy and would always sleep on my pillow, and after he passed away, I missed that so very much. My pillow now feels very bare without him purring in my ear. I will never forget him and how much he meant to me.

He was the one that started my obsession with cats and so our house now always has a cat, and currently, we have three! We have two tabby cats and a ragdoll cat. They are all special in their own way, and they have a place in my heart, but there will always be a hole where Jasper had been. Jasper knew how to calm me when I needed it most, and he was the therapy I needed without me realising it. I still remember the day before he passed away. Jasper lay in my lap for almost the entire day as if to say his final farewell. I love my other cats, but Jasper was the hardest to let go...

Recently I went through a midlife burnout due to wearing myself too thin, trying to be more than I could be and taking on too much in life. Losing Jasper added to it. After working in my own photography business for many years, photographing both families and pets, life started to fall apart. I lost my passion for many things that year, but it was also the year I took up writing again. It helped with some of my healing and working through my emotions.

It wasn't until one of my children was diagnosed with autism at the age of seven in 2011, that I started to see a lot of myself in him and realised that I might be autistic too. It was a lightbulb moment as I came to that realisation. One of the great things about Facebook is the ability to find a community of other women that either self-identified or were diagnosed. The more I spoke with them, the more I began to make sense of who I was, and it all started to come together. After a lot of research, I sought out a clinical psychologist who specialised in the assessment of women on the autism spectrum. In late 2015 I received my autism diagnosis and breathed out a long breath of relief.

Once I had the diagnosis even though I knew in my mind that I was autistic, the diagnosis made it more real to me. It wasn't just in my head, and I began to understand myself better. I felt validated. I was also able to be more forgiving when I became overwhelmed or felt caught in awkward situations such as misunderstanding social cues. For the first time, I thought it was okay to ask for support, and I felt brave enough to seek out help. It helped to explain why I did some of the things that I do.

It was a relief to take a step back from running my business in the same year that I received my diagnosis. I loved meeting all the families and animals that I photographed, but I had lost the passion, especially with the business side of things, and felt that I needed to look after myself for a time. I have no regrets in the time I spent on my business, nor letting go of it either.

My eldest son was pleased to hear I had autism like him. I've always taught him to be accepting of who he is and to be proud of being autistic. If we weren't autistic, we wouldn't be who we are. Of course, we have our struggles, and sometimes those struggles can put us in very dark places, but we also have our strengths, and with support and acceptance we can be the people we want and strive to be.

These days I spend much time writing when not caring for my children. Writing epic fantasy has always been my favourite genre. My current manuscript involves a cat (no surprise there!), a princess and all the magic you can muster, along with wizards, warriors and a magic book.

I also recently became employed working in a field that I am very passionate about - the NDIS (National Disability Insurance Scheme). I work with a provider who offers plan management to NDIS participants, and I'm happy to be working for a company that is disability- and family-inclusive and helps those that have barriers (like myself) to gain employment which makes us feel appreciated for the skills and knowledge we can share. It has opened up many opportunities for me and others like me who have many obstacles when it comes to employment.

I am open about my diagnosis, and I'm passionate about my autistic identity because it is a huge part of who I am. It is how I feel and see the world.

I don't believe autism is something to be ashamed of and have shared this on my writer's page, as well as with friends and family. I hope that I can give that acceptance to others and let them know that it's okay to be yourself. I'm autistic, but I'm also a writer, a reader, a wife, a mother, a photographer and a cat lover. These are all parts of me just as much as how my brain is wired. I don't want to be an inspiration just for the fact that I am autistic and can do everyday things I would like to inspire others to be accepting of differences and that it's okay just to be you. I would like to encourage others to read my stories and perhaps write for themselves one day. This is how I would like to inspire.

Remember, no one can be better at being you than yourself, and that is a good way to be.

EIGHT

Our Journey with James
by Cristina Lantican Rodert

LIFE IS NOT MEANT TO BE EASY! IN 1994 AS AN OVERSEAS student in Adelaide, South Australia, I was very lonely, but things changed when I met and married Kym. Then along came James. Everything could have been well and good, but James is a 'special' child—challenging and difficult, but also rewarding and fulfilling at the same time. Soon our lives revolved around him.

Our motto: *When James is happy, we are all happy.*

Over the years, South Australia has grown on me, and it is now the place I call home.

Our baby
James was born seven weeks early at the Women's and Children's Hospital in Adelaide, a very tiny 1.74 kg (3.84 lb) baby with Down Syndrome. The average birth weight for babies is around 3.5 kg (7.5 lb). James was so little we couldn't even find clothes for him,

so he wore doll clothes. He stayed in the hospital for two months so he could have two major operations. First, the duodenal atresia surgery repaired the blockage in his stomach, and then the ASD/VSD (atrial septal defect and ventral septal defect) operation closed the holes in his heart. During this time, I stayed in the hospital sitting next to his cot, oblivious of the people around me. I stared helplessly at James with all the tubes attached to his body. He looked so tiny, sick and fragile. There was nothing I could do but hold him in my arms, as much as his condition would permit.

Early days
Once James was discharged from the hospital, I stayed home to care for him. When James was four months old, he had pneumococcal meningitis, and he spent over a week in the hospital. About that time, we noticed that James did not respond to sounds or noises around him and he was later diagnosed with a hearing loss in both ears. We attempted to fit James with hearing aids, but they never stayed on for any more than two minutes at a time. After trying for two years, we finally gave up. Due to his hearing loss, James has never spoken a single word.

We received early intervention support from the Department of Education, and we received numerous supports to get James ready to go to school. The Down Syndrome Society and the Special Education Resource Unit of the Department of Education regularly saw James. The occupational therapists from the Department of Communities and Social Inclusion also visited James at home. We had visits from the mobile toy library that loaned us toys, and had visitors almost every week. Keeping the appointment-calendar organised was exhausting. Although the services and the support that came with them, was appreciated, I often felt invaded with so many people coming to our home.

James had a fairly normal life at home except for the regular trips to the Women's and Children's Hospital for monthly specialist consultations. James got sick very easily, so there were many trips to our local surgery. We used a humidifier in his room to ease his breathing since he had numerous colds. Due to his weak immune system, he required the influenza vaccine every year.

When James was two years old, our daughter Hannah was born. James adored her and always wanted to play with her. Unfortunately, he was very rough and often, unknowingly, hurt her. I had to watch James like a hawk all the time and not leave Hannah alone with him. He also had no concept of dangers around him, so we needed to lock everything. He needed to be supervised at all times while playing. Instead of taking care of the housework, I was focused on looking after James and keeping Hannah safe.

Children love to go to the park, so we went often, but James played too roughly with children smaller than himself. So we went early in the morning, sometimes as early as 6 am. The play equipment was still wet with morning dew, so I had to bring a towel to wipe everything dry. Once other families started arriving, it was time for us to go. I had to keep an eye on James all the time making sure that he did not run away. Seeing James and Hannah having fun at the park made it worthwhile going through all the hassles to get there. James screaming with joy is a delight to see and hear.

Delays

When James started walking at two years old, we were happy and developed a manageable routine with eating, playing and sleeping. However, toileting became a big issue due to his developmental delay and medical conditions. We tried many strategies to get him toilet-trained using cue cards, rewards, stickers and signs but nothing worked. He would do little, if anything, in the toilet. He would not sit. He would grab our hair, or do his business on the floor, or somewhere else. We had no success.

James was non-verbal so communicating with him was a challenge and we relied on visual cues and sign language. One of the hardest parts of caring for James was when he was unwell because it was difficult to know what was wrong. We didn't know what he was wanting or thinking.

Personal care

James does not want anything in his mouth, and he will fight with all his might to stop someone from getting into his mouth, so he does not brush his teeth. Most of his dental appointments have been unsuccessful. It is a waste of our time to go when he doesn't open his mouth for the dentist. We ensure that James does not eat any lollies or sweet things and give him healthy food. He also does not eat nuts or anything that can get stuck in his teeth. We get him to bath/shower so at least his mouth can be cleaned by water before bed.

James used to attend day surgery once a year to clean his ears and check his teeth at the Women's and Children's Hospital. This was meant to be a thirty-minute procedure. However, we stayed in the hospital for half a day as James was given a general anaesthetic. We felt helpless about this, but at least he received the care he needed. Since James turned eighteen, the services from the Women's and Children's Hospital stopped, and we were referred to the Royal Adelaide Hospital. We are still waiting to hear back for James to be seen by a specialist. Meantime, James is being seen by regular general practitioners as required.

When James was little, I was able to cut his hair with scissors, but he started resisting as he got older and stronger. There were times when I was unable to finish his haircut in one session, so I had to finish it the following week. It was the same with cutting his nails. Kym and I had to wrestle to get James' nails cut. There were times I sneaked into my sleeping son's room to finish his haircut or nails cut. In the dark, with Hannah holding the torch, snip, snip. I had to do this as quietly as I could. It worked for a while, but James got very sensitive and started to wake up every time.

Growing up
Growing up, James ate a minimal range of food, so I had stocks of James' preferred food in the house. Running out was disastrous and frustrating for James and often led to violence. When James wanted something, he wanted it now! I had to attend to him regardless of what I was doing. There were times my coffee got cold, and dinner had to wait. If I was sick or unwell, too bad, I had to get up.

James has always loved Vegemite sandwiches, so there was always a cupboard full of Vegemite. The only fruit that James would eat was grapes. We bought them when in season and off season, whether they were $2/kilo or $20/kilo. It never mattered how much. We had to buy grapes!

James also loved the 'Original Kettle Chips' which was another staple in our cupboard. When we were running low on Kettle Chips, no one would be allowed to eat them until we re-stocked. I made trips to supermarkets early in the morning or late at night to re-stock his Kettle Chips. They made great birthday presents from friends and families.

Our family was able to manage James at home when he was young, but as he got older and bigger, the challenges increased. Looking after James was full on. He was always on the move, and always needing supervision. James could not sit still for ten seconds. At home, he would go in and out of the door more than a hundred times. We could hear the door banging every five seconds. It drove us nuts. We had to keep our gate shut with the padlock all the time, and every cupboard had a locking mechanism so that James could not open them. Even our key safe had its own key.

The banging was constant, but this gave me comforting thoughts that James was engaged. I got frantic sometimes when the banging stopped, thinking that something might have happened to James or he might have escaped out of the gate.

Sleeping was another issue. James stayed up late and woke up in the middle of the night, every night. He would wake up at 3 am and not want to go back to bed again. Someone had to get up to keep an eye on him. This significantly impacted our family and our work. My husband and I were exhausted during the day, due to stress and lack of sleep.

James has behavioural issues and can be violent at times, especially when things don't go his way. Dealing with him on a daily basis is a monumental task, emotionally stressful and physically draining. Just the simple chore of cooking, which I truly enjoy, can be stressful when James is around the kitchen. We put a gate in the kitchen, but as he got older, it became easy for him to get through the gate. At meal times James would throw our plates away, and we had to hang on to our plates. We used unbreakable plastic plates in case James got hold of them.

Hanging the washing with James around can be very tricky as he likes tipping the peg basket over, again and again. I have to hang the clothes while holding on to the peg basket.

Despite all the challenges, Kym and I tried our best to be positive and celebrate every little win. We loved to watch James line up his toys in the chairs so that he could perform for them. I learned to savour each opportunity to drink hot coffee and relish any bedtime earlier than 11 pm. I appreciate simple things in life such as being able to cook uninterrupted, to hang the washing in peace or being able to sit and rest for longer than five minutes. We cherish each day that James is happy and well.

School

James went to kindy at Mt Barker then went to the Mt Barker Primary School where he was supported in their special unit. We wanted James to go to St Michael's Lutheran School in Hahndorf. Due to his high needs, we were advised that the school would not be able to support him. James went to Mt Barker Primary School for a few months but due to being unable to support his high needs, he transferred to the Murray Bridge Special School.

A taxi picked him up in the morning and dropped him off in the afternoon. This routine went well for a couple of years until James got bored and started misbehaving in the taxi. He would strip off his clothes, take off his seat belt and throw things at the driver. Immediately, we started using a seat belt buckle guard. Then we introduced a series of things for James to play with to keep him entertained: lemons, which he eventually threw at the driver, a bead necklace that the school vetoed as a choking hazard, and 'Chewlery' (safe and non-toxic jewellery) which was great until the expense of replacement became too high.

I started working part-time when Hannah began school. It was very hectic as every morning I had to get James ready for the taxi pick up, drop Hannah off to school, and then go to work. The tricky part was picking Hannah up at the same time as James was being dropped off by the taxi at home. It was always a racing game and there were times on the road when I saw his taxi; I would try to beat it by taking shortcuts.

After four years at the Murray Bridge Special School, we transferred James to Ashford Special School to get closer to the Women's and Children's Hospital so that it would be easier to attend specialist appointments. We were very happy with the school, and the staff were fantastic.

Diagnosis

James would often sit crossed-legged and rock himself backwards and forward, but it wasn't until he was twelve that he was diagnosed with autism.

James' behavioural issues continued as he was growing up and we tried our best to manage the everyday challenges. I was always alert, on the ball and it seemed like I had eyes in the back of my head when looking after James. My patience was at its best. He started taking five different medications. We would dress him, bathe him, prepare his food, supervise him all the time and do just about everything for him. It was a challenge. He was so dependent on us.

Due to the complexity of caring for James, our daughter Hannah missed out on our attention. She couldn't participate in sports or attend her friends' parties. She couldn't invite her friends for sleepovers due to James' behavioural issues. More than that, we could not entertain friends or family at our home or attend their gatherings due to our caring responsibilities. We could not take James to other people's houses due to his unacceptable social behaviour. We became isolated from family and our social network.

Destruction

James wrecked many things at home. He broke our windows so many times that we had Perspex windows installed. These are durable, and even though he has banged and scratched them more than a thousand times, they are still unbroken. He has also broken plates and glasses. One time he picked up a stack of plates and just dropped them on the floor. That is when we put up the kitchen gate and purchased plastic plates.

James has an iPad which he uses to watch music and videos. When I bought an iPad for myself, he wanted the new one instead. Due to his inability to express his wants verbally, he stabbed his own device with a screwdriver. I got it fixed, but he did it again, and only then did I realise that he wanted my new iPad.

When James sat on the door of our new oven, the supplier fixed the door, feeling sorry for us, but advised that it would not be fixed again. But of course, James sat on the oven door again, and Kym had to fix it by putting a hinge on it. I put up with an oven that did not seal properly for over ten years until we replaced it very recently.

Our 63" plasma 3D television lasted eight months before James hammered the screen. When we replaced it, Kym boxed it in so James could not reach it. I am thankful for Kym's woodworking and handyman skills that enable him to build things to meet James' needs.

James has broken so many mobile phones and radios that I have lost track. It was costly but James loves to listen to music so it's worth it. We share his joy each time we see him happy, listening to his music.

Accidents

As you can imagine, our watchfulness sometimes failed, but James taught us the hard way. Once James escaped out of our gate on his trike. He fell alongside the road, scraped his cheek and injured himself. As a reminder, he has a scar below his nose telling us to keep our gate shut at all times.

Another time, James sat on the lawn mower that was so hot that he burnt his left leg leaving another big scar. He also burned his arm on the stove. It was hard to know which section of his arm was burnt, but when the blister showed, it was a large section, which left a huge scar on his arm.

The biggest accident of all involved cutting off three fingers with a circular saw. Kym was cutting some wood and put the circular saw on the ground, James picked it up and tried to use it accidentally cutting his three fingers. Hannah frantically rang the ambulance. She phoned me at work, and I rushed to get home. Kym and I spent the next three days and two sleepless nights in the hospital with James.

With all the accidents comes blood, but that doesn't faze James at all. He is prone to blood noses with extreme temperature changes. I get frantic and try to clean him up, but he doesn't care and will keep blowing his nose until there is blood everywhere.

In 2012, James had to undergo surgery to remove a growth on his ear. When he was taken back to the ward, he was agitated and unwrapped his bandage. He banged himself on the wall making his incision bleed. I tried to wipe his blood, but he was so agitated that I have to leave his face full of blood. I knelt on the floor crying and upset, feeling helpless, not knowing what to do. We were supposed to stay overnight in the hospital, but due to James' anxiety, the doctor decided to discharge James early. We had to sign a document stating that he was being released against medical advice. In the comfort of our home, James slept well that night. Next day we worked hard to keep James busy. We went for a long ride in the car. His face and ear were all covered in dry blood, but we didn't want to cause more bleeding with his raw scar. So the blood stayed there until he could settle down.

Respite

As James approached puberty, his behavioural issues continued to escalate. His violence at home became unbearable and the sleepless nights continued. He started staying at the respite home when he was twelve years old. It was a very difficult, heart-breaking decision for our family to make, but it was the only way we would be able to function. At fifteen years of age, he stayed full time at Minda Housing's supported accommodation. James now comes home one night a week. We finally found a happy balance.

With James living at the supported accommodation, our daughter Hannah was finally able to participate in sports and to play netball. She could invite her friends home for sleepovers and to take part in extra-curricular after school activities. We grieved over sending James to Minda. However, we had to let go so that James could be the best person that he can be.

James has become independent since he started living at Minda full time. But due to his inability to communicate, he sometimes still expresses his frustrations in violent and unacceptable ways. In the beginning, he went through a phase where he ripped his clothes. We were unsure what triggered this behaviour and were unable to stop it. All I could do was to keep buying and supplying new clothes for James each week. This was an expensive exercise that went on for several months.

James was fifteen years old when he was finally toilet-trained. Also, at respite, James discovered that other kids ate a variety of food, so he started to follow their example. Now he enjoys a much healthier diet. We are grateful to the staff for their great efforts to lead James towards independence. These are significant achievements and huge milestones.

The transport schedule for James' weekly visits home from Minda was organised for the whole term so I needed to anticipate all family events so that James could enjoy them. I had to plan three months ahead for Mother's Day, Father's Day and birthdays. Changing the schedule and transportation arrangement was stressful and required lots of paperwork from the school, so I always tried to get it right from the very beginning.

James is always busy when he is at home. I cannot imagine where he gets all his energy from. He's so strong and such a busy young man who will hardly sit still for a minute. He is always on the go. He is constantly in and out of the front and back doors.

The future

James is a happy, fun loving person who lives life without having to worry about anything, as long as he gets what he wants. His life is straightforward and includes his love of music, dancing and performing. James loves having concerts where he dances and sings in his own ways. He is really a joy to watch. We love and adore him so much.

Life is unpredictable, but I have taken the challenge face on. I say, 'Bring it on!' I try my best to stay positive, but there are days when I'm just close to breaking down. There are times I'm unable to cope, but I have to be strong. There's no one else or nowhere else to go. I have to keep strong for the sake of our family.

But don't get me wrong; while life with James can be tiring and challenging, I'm not complaining. We all have our own baggage to carry, and mine happens to be my son. James has changed my perspective on life. I have learned to appreciate the small things. James filled a void in our family; he completed us. James is the centre of our universe. If James is happy, we're all happy.

I am very grateful to the Australian Government for supporting people with disabilities like James. He enjoys a very good quality of life, and he is well cared for at Minda. Looking into the future, we hope that James continues to be supported at Minda. We cannot look after James forever, and we are comforted by the thought that he is in a safe, secure environment. Our hope for James is for him to reach his full potential, be happy, healthy and well looked after.

NINE

The Obstacle Course

by Ross Hill-Brown and John Francis

Psalm 66:12
'... we went through fire and through water: but thou broughtest us out into a wealthy place.'
King James Version (KJV)

IT COULD HAVE BEEN SAID I HAD MY ACCIDENT JUST SO I COULD stay longer in the UK, to watch the 2015 Rugby World Cup. Such a thought appeals to my cynical sense of humour, however untrue it might have been.

Why, and how the car I was driving, with my mother alongside me and my brother in the back, drifted across the middle line I guess I will never know.

What I do know is that it happened during a series of events, one of which remains unfinished as I write. What follows then is a story about faith, hope, generosity and love from others as well as great medical staff and, in no small measure, my own part in it.

I can be tough. On myself, and with others, including my own family. During my first few months in hospital, I was incredibly calm. My wife Joy said, 'why can't you be like that all the time?' I'm short-tempered. I can get very, very angry. I'll fly off the handle, then suddenly let it go. I'm also stubborn, and single-minded. I pretend that taking part is more important than winning, but I do not always practise this mantra when competing. I'm sure, though, these quirks helped me through the tough times.

At times I can be quite emotional—it is not unknown for a tear or two to be shed during a movie for instance. I can turn the waterworks on and let out the emotion. It's a good thing, I think, not to bottle things up.

I've certainly shed a few tears over this journey to recovery—some from sadness, some from frustration, and some from the joy of success.

I was born in 1955 and brought up in the small seaside resort of Swanage, Dorset, in the UK. I am the eldest of three boys. The next youngest is intellectually disabled. My youngest is a Church of England minister. The church has always been a feature of my life.

My working life has been spent largely in policing. I was many years in the Royal Hong Kong Police. I retired from that force as a Chief Inspector, at the time Britain handed over Hong Kong to China in 1997.

In Hong Kong, I was more hands-on than some of the others, even as I went up the ranks. I hated being in the office, preferring to be out with the troops. I gained two commendations this way. I'm a people person, and a team player. Being grumpy and with a short fuse, I had troops who loved me, but others who hated me. Despite my flaws, I think many understood that they could rely on me to support them and that I would always go into bat for them.

I was also something of a rebel. Colonial Hong Kong had a paramilitary police force. This meant when an officer did something wrong, they could find themselves before a disciplinary hearing. I would often represent them. This wasn't good for my career because I wasn't toeing the party line, but I felt it was important.

Being prepared to be different and think outside the box is also an important trait for an intelligence analyst. So it was setting me up for my future career.

I've also been a very active athlete. I've won a couple of sashes in pro running: gold silver and bronze at national level Masters, and bronze in the Police-Fire World Games four-by-four relay. Leading up to my accident I had also competed in the sixty to sixty-four age group in the state, national and world Masters' events.

Back in 1993, four years before leaving Hong Kong, my now long-suffering wife, Joy, and I had married. After Hong Kong, we moved to Australia. We bought a house in the Adelaide Hills, and I eventually found work as a security guard/cleaner. Joy, who has chronic fatigue, taught for the Dyslexia and Specific Learning Difficulties Association of South Australia. Later I joined the state government as Sheriff's Officer and then in 1999 became an Intelligence Analyst with South Australia Police. I'm still in that role, as I write. In February 2001, our son Daniel was born,

It was just before Christmas 2014, when the chain of events started. Joy was on the phone to her sister in the UK, discussing the condition of her ninety-three-year-old mother, who had ovarian cancer. Joy and her sister got onto the subject of symptoms. This prompted Joy to go the next day to the doctor, and to find she had breast cancer.

That night Joy phoned her mum with the news. I wonder now, had her mother been holding on, expecting her daughter over shortly to see her, but now feeling there was no point? At any rate, Joy's mother died that night.

Joy hurried over for the funeral. A week later, back in Adelaide, the first stage of her own treatment began, with the removal of her left breast and a number of lymph nodes. Chemo started soon after.

We had been planning, as a family, to visit the UK the following Christmas. With Joy's ongoing treatment, it was now uncertain if she would be able to travel. It was agreed though that I should visit my elderly mum, during our winter of 2015.

I was a member of the SA Masters Athletic Club. I persuaded Joy to let me have an extra week away to represent Australia at the World Masters Track and Field in Lyon, France, in the sixty to sixty-four age class. The intention was for me to be back before the start of her radiation treatment.

I spent two lovely weeks with my mother before heading to France at the beginning of August.

On 12 August I ran a four hundred metre heat. I did quite well in Australian terms, but since I didn't progress to the finals, I left Lyon on Saturday 15 August to spend a few more days with my mother.

By the Sunday afternoon, I was an incomplete tetraplegic. And my mother was no more.

≈

On a Sunday drive with Mum and Andrew, my brother, I somehow crossed the white line and hit a car on the other side of the road. Why? I have no idea. Speed, drugs or alcohol were ruled out.

As I started to come around, I could hear the moans of my brother in the back seat. I was less than sympathetic, suggesting things were not that bad. I also have a surreal memory of Mum.

I'm not sure if she was talking at that point, but later, apparently, she was chatting away saying how lovely it was to 'have her boys home'. They say she seemed in good spirits. Once removed from the car, she would die of major trauma.

In my case, I remember there were a lot of people milling around, holding my hand and encouraging me. I have no memory of getting out of the car.

Based on my medical notes, I had suffered severe bruising to vertebrae three to seven in my cervical spine. I was airlifted to Poole General Hospital while my brother was airlifted to Southampton General Hospital with a life-threatening ruptured spleen and a back injury. I have a recollection at Poole Hospital of police officers visiting me to tell me of my mother's passing. I think by then my aunt (my father's sister) had arrived to see me.

I spent the night in ICU and have few memories except of the MRI. It was my first such experience, and after about twenty minutes I freaked out. They pulled me out, only to tell me if I had hung on, I might have only spent about another five minutes in that 'tomb'. As it was, I had to go back for at least another ten minutes.

Later I remember the doctor saying I was likely to spend the rest of my life paralysed.

The next day it was decided I should join my brother in Southampton Hospital, which was better-equipped to handle my type of injuries. This meant a thirty-two-mile ambulance journey. I had a police escort, a doctor and two nurses and was ensconced in a type of air cushion. The journey seemed to go on forever, and I just wanted it to end. I've since learnt from a retired Hong Kong Police friend, who has done such escorts, that speed of transfer is not the issue. The aim is to minimise movement and swaying.

At Southampton, I became an expert in identifying different patterns on the ceiling as I was on flat bed rest for six weeks. There were triangular cuts, dots, stripes and paint blobs. The ceilings on the lower floors were painted, brighter and in much better condition than my eventual wards on F level.

In ICU they operated and placed two rods in my neck. After about six days my Assistant Commissioner of Police from South Australia, who just happened to be in England for a wedding, paid a visit. After this, my family tells me they noticed a considerable improvement in my recovery. Also around this time, on the day of my mother's funeral, my youngest brother, Duncan, arranged for a minister friend of his to visit. So we two hospitalised brothers said prayers and read scripture—and ate a cake baked by my mother before she died.

It was many months before I watched the actual service on DVD, in the hospital chapel with Duncan. He had been planning a sabbatical with his family to visit us in Adelaide and see Australia for the first time. Instead, he was chasing about the country for Andrew and me and sorting out my mother's funeral and her estate. The strange thing about being the injured one is that it's far harder on those who have to pick up the pieces.

I also remember while in ICU being visited by a guy in a wheelchair from the UK Spinal Injury Association. The idea was to assure me that I could survive in a wheelchair. In all honesty I think it just made me determined that I was going to walk out of rehab on my two feet.

While Duncan had to wear everything, and Joy back in Australia was undergoing her treatment and worrying how things would work out, I was in an absurdly calm place. The hospital chaplaincy assisted greatly in this. That's not to say I didn't easily break down, mainly when talking about my mother's passing. Or when trying to fathom out why the accident occurred.

I had to be fed, clothed, turned every two hours which made sleep difficult, completely assisted with toiletry, have others blow my nose or have them remove hairs from my face. I didn't even have the strength to press the buzzer for assistance. These days I can get very frustrated when I can't do simple things like undoing shirt buttons. Yet during that period when I could do so little, I felt a sort of calm wellbeing.

The most important thing each day was my phone call from home. As I had little movement in my hands, I had to shout for someone to pick up the phone and hold it to my ear.

By the time I left ICU, I had movement in my legs, mainly the right one. I remember once speaking to our son Daniel, in the early days of ICU, telling him I could move my right leg a bit and him replying at least I could take part in hopping races. I had a little movement in my right arm, but only a finger and thumb worked on the left.

My first ward at this time had windows that looked out to the building next door and was stiflingly hot. I was only there for five days, but the other patients were great fun to be with.

It was also where Andrew had been treated, and he had fond memories of it, later visiting the staff whenever he came to see me. Early in November, he moved into a flat on his own for the first time in his life. With the help of professional carers and family support, he seems to have settled down well.

From September to just after Christmas I was in the one ward, F4, and so got to know the kind and supportive staff very well. Patients here were generally in for short-stay knee and hip replacements. I met many new people. One of my fellow patients was involved in criminal intelligence analysis with the Dorset police. His wife also worked for them. She was in the police control room when my accident occurred. Later, in another ward and just before leaving, I met another criminal intelligence analyst. We are a unique bunch.

Once out of ICU I started to get more and more assistance from the physios and occupational therapists.

Then came a series of non-medical roadblocks.

In early October they started to let me sit up a little and I was being promised a transfer to a rehab unit in Salisbury. My surgeon even said to make sure my bags were ready and packed. But it was never going to happen. Even up to the start of November, I was still hoping. But no. It was just one of a string of bureaucrat-driven frustrations. The most serious being financial.

Despite being a dual British-Australian citizen holding a British National Health Service (NHS) number, they denied me funding on the ground that I did not intend to take up residence in the country after finishing my in-house rehab. So I languished in a hospital system not geared for long-term patients. While the 'system' seemed immovable, the professionals who cared for me were exemplary. They offered me everything that was available. I had gym, hydro as well as many exercise machines around my bed. The dedication of these wonderful people paid off. But I think, equally, they were surprised with the outcomes.

My physio team, whose leader used my progress for a case study, honestly believed the best they could achieve in hydro would be to have me lowered into the water and float about. However, on 5 November an event happened that left me flowing with tears: I stood for ten seconds. My whole body was alive with emotion. This, I could see, would be the start of my real journey.

By December, I had stopped relying on hoists and was even starting to walk a few steps. On days like this, when I was pushing myself to go one step further, I would scare the physios. One day, though, I was the frightened one. The physio team were daring me into taking steps unaided for the first time. And even more than that, to catch balls. Challenges like this took me to the edge of the cliff, but they also achieved the required response. I continued to go beyond whatever they confronted me with. In many ways, it was no different to preparing for a championship sprint. However, I do feel my progress was miraculous.

Life still had its stumbles. For each physical step forward it seemed, there would be two financial steps back.

It wasn't just the NHS not coming to the party. My travel insurance company also did everything to avoid paying my planned medical evacuation back to Australia. I was also under a cloud of potential criminal proceedings, with the UK Coroner wanting to interview me under caution over my mother's death. To my enormous relief, thanks to the common sense of the police officer investigating the matter, this didn't eventuate.

Then there was my wife Joy. One day I got worried because she hadn't phoned. Eventually, I was told she had gone to hospital, with a severe case of vertigo. She had been under so much emotional pressure from the worry caused by the stone-walling of the insurance company. Vertigo is now an ongoing problem for Joy.

The frustrations over that hoped-for move to the rehab unit in Salisbury also continued. I remember late one Friday evening getting a call which was an attempt to trap me into saying that after treatment I would return to Australia. I broke down in tears over that and asked the ward sister to intervene with any further communications. In the end, there was no Salisbury special unit move. Instead, it was agreed that after rehab I could stay with Duncan, whose house was deemed suitable for someone in a wheelchair, even though I had vowed to walk out of rehab on my two feet.

It was all set then, it seemed. Before Christmas, I would go for rehab in Oswestry, which was near Birmingham, where Duncan lived. All seemed ready, with reports written by my surgeon and physio—and then two days after Joy had arrived in the UK, on 7 December, the NHS announced its final decision —no, it would not fund me.

The uncertainty leading up to this had meant my wife and son had had no idea where they would stay on arriving in the UK. In the end, they stayed with my uncle who lived about an hour away from the hospital by train.

The irony of Joy visiting is that my solo visit to England had been arranged because we thought, with Joy's cancer treatment, she would not have been able to travel for our planned holiday trip here the following Christmas. By this stage in her treatment, however, she had been on Herceptin since October and her doctor felt confident that she could go a month rather than a normal fortnight between sessions.

A surprise was planned for Joy and Daniel's arrival in my ward. They were unaware that I had started to walk a few steps with a frame. So before they arrived the staff hustled me out so I could walk back and surprise them. It was a teary reunion. The relief of at last being together again was mixed with the reality of Joy's and my medical situations. But at least we were together.

Over the time Joy and Daniel were with me I got stronger, either walking or propelling myself further in the wheelchair each day. One regular activity was wheeling me to the only nearby green space, a large municipal cemetery. All rugged up for the cold I loved those outings, being able to hear the birds and breathe fresh air. We also discovered little outdoor gardens scattered around the hospital. However, the most tranquil spot was the chapel.

The chaplaincy supported my recovery in such a big way. There were the Sunday chapel services, and the carol service with its magnificent and scented real tree at Christmas was a very uplifting experience. I looked forward to regular bedside visits from the chaplains. They would often read to me from my daily readings written by Max Lucado. So often, that day's reading would hit the mood and inspire. It was very much part of my road to recovery.

I was also helped by all the wonderful visits from family and friends, often from people I hadn't seen for many years. My uncle, who lived nearby, was a regular and arranged things such as talking books to keep me entertained. I listened to the whole history of the Boer War, amongst other things.

From mid-November, family and friends had been taking me down to the canteen. These were days I really looked forward to, as it got me out of the ward. While Joy and Daniel were with me, I had even more opportunities to head to the canteen, for alternatives to the ward food.

There had in fact, even from my early days in hospital, been a variety of treats from family and friends. A retired Chinese Police colleague brought lovely fried rice. Soon after I'd left ICU, my wife had notified my old police association, and many had come to pay visits. One regularly offered to do my laundry as I started to dress more and more in my own clothes. When it was thought the insurance company would not pay up, the association explored ways it might help. One of my old bosses visited, flying over from Portugal where he now lived. It upset one of the more sensitive nurses when he was overheard to say on his phone, 'must break off now as I have to feed a cripple'. I knew he was joking, but this nurse approached me the next day asking who the 'terrible man' was.

The hospital food was repetitive. It's designed for short stay patients, not those who get stuck in the system for seven months. It made one of the patient's wife's offers of 'bacon butties' very special. Another patient was a retired Cunard chef who had been a consultant to one of the NHS hospitals. He pointed out it would be very easy to make the food much more interesting, for little extra cost.

As I'm not the most even-tempered person at times, food matters brought my blood to boiling point on several occasions. From early in my long hospital stay I was able to order one meal a day from the canteen. Sometimes this order would just not go through. One of my old police colleagues, the one who did my laundry, was with me on such an occasion. I made sufficient fuss to have the duty manager come to see me. He blamed it on a communication breakdown. This did not go down well with two retired chief inspectors who were used to having command over up to a hundred personnel. As we explained to the canteen manager, telling our superintendents or for that matter the public, that our police operation went wrong because we were unable to clearly explain instructions to our staff, would have meant transfers or facing a disciplinary hearing. Another time I was falsely told I had refused to give an order. Had I been physically able to get up from my wheelchair the consequences might not have gone well. This time the supervisor was very soothing and apologetic and made every effort to get me something different.

It was unfortunate that my wife and uncle were visiting when I had one such outburst. They were concerned by what they saw as my violent overreaction. Especially as I had, in the weeks and even months leading up to this, appeared so calm and satisfied with life. Sometimes I wish that the 'new me' of that period could have lasted a lot longer.

Flat on one's back has its compensations when one is in the country hosting the Rugby World Cup. Also over this time, the Poms met Australia in the semi-final of the Davis Cup.

Joy and Daniel left after we had celebrated Christmas and my birthday at the hospital. At both celebrations, we had a number of family members from both sides. Christmas lunch in the canteen was not bad, and we had special sandwiches in the ward for tea. My ward was at a high enough level to get a good view of the fireworks both at Christmas and New Year, and both were quite spectacular. By that time I was allowed a can of Guinness each day as my iron levels were low.

With Joy gone, positive moves began towards my medical evacuation. About three weeks before I left, I moved wards. That ward was nearer a small hospital café, about 200 metres from my bed. One of my goals, which I managed to achieve, was to walk there with my stick on my own, to buy myself a treat.

On Saturday 30 January 2016 an evacuation nurse arrived from Australia. The next day I was wheeled down to where a limousine was waiting to take us to the airport. At the door I got up from my wheelchair and walked down the ramp, fulfilling my goal to walk out of hospital unaided.

The Australian rehab unit had suggested I be fitted with a catheter for the flight home. I fought against this. I'd had two urinary infections caused by them, and never wanted to have another. Urinary infections and spinal injuries are not uncommon and before antibiotics, the infections led to the death of many.

Hampstead, the rehab unit operated by the Royal Adelaide Hospital, has an incredibly experienced and competent rehabilitation consultant, who has built up a very strong and loyal team. I only stayed there a month, but through the team she has put together I, and many others, have been able to make such good recoveries. The most outstanding member of this exceptional team was the head of physical training, who has been in a wheelchair since a teen and had been a Paralympian in both basketball and wheelchair racing. With his incredible upper body strength he was able, from his wheelchair, to push us up hills in ours.

Through exercise and medicines, after that one month I was able to leave Hampstead and come home. I continued therapy first at home and then through the now-closed Repatriation Hospital, and in the hydro pool at Flinders Hospital. At Flinders I trained with one of our Paralympian rowers. Oh yes, I love to brag about that! I now do some neuro Pilates and gym work.

I'm so fortunate to have my life back. But yes, it is a modified style of living.

Joy, Daniel and I went on a cruise this year. I felt older. Before the accident I could have run up fifteen decks. Not now. Yesterday I even fell over, something I've never done before. And it's a slow process to get up...I cannot do buttons without a special little hook. Even then I need help to do my top button and cuffs.

Joy has been diagnosed with chronic fatigue since our coming to Australia. After the accident she wrote saying, 'I gather you'll be doing things at my pace now'. I used to bring her a morning cup of tea. I'm still coming to terms with tasks I did around the house and am no longer able or allowed to do. I can't help much in the garden. I can do a bit of cooking, but it takes a lot longer. Peeling carrots for instance I use a special peeling board, and I take twice as long as my wife.

In October 2017 I returned to a level of competitive sport—mostly race walking, but in November of that year I sort of ran a one hundred metres for the first time—at about the speed of an eighty-five-year-old, at 39.4 seconds.

Milestones have included attending the Athletics Classic as an invited VIP, being able to contribute to some household chores like washing up, making my bed, and when the mood takes me, cleaning the bathroom basin. And of course, no longer being within the institutional confines of hospitals. There was the emotional experience of going to my and my wife's churches to thank the congregations for their prayers and support. It has been such a relief to get my old roles back, for instance sitting on the Mitcham Hill's Inter-church Council, and helping out at the Masters' Athletics at the 2016 National Track and Field Championships in Adelaide.

My old athletics club, Flinders, elected me vice-president and as their representative to Athletics SA. I've attended a number of meetings and had the chance to drum the cause of older para sportspeople.

In July 2016 there was the challenge of returning to my old job, first for a few hours a week and now full-time. The following year I got a new adapted automatic Mazda 2, which has given me back much of my independence and is easing some of my wife's 'taxi driver' responsibilities for both me and my son.

Having an accident like mine, I appreciate being at work. I want to be there. I value that opportunity, and the importance of it to my wellbeing.

The joys outnumber the regrets. It's actually harder for the others in my life. They suffer more than the victim, doing the running around, and worrying.

So this has been my journey. I don't intend to preach, but I genuinely believe my miraculous recovery has been down to the power of prayer of those who are much more worthy of God's love than myself. As Paul says in the letter to the Philippians 1:6, 'he … hath begun a good work in you ….' (KJV). That is not to say I have not been blessed by some very able people in the medical profession and a faithful family and supportive workplace. However, I still believe it has been by the grace of God I am where I am today, for which I give thanks.

I did think about acknowledging all who helped but I know I will hurt someone by leaving them out, so I will just conclude by thanking all those who sent emails, all those who supported Joy, all those who visited me while in hospital, who travelled many miles from overseas including to Australia, my surgical team and its support staff, all the nurses, physios, occupational therapists, gymnasium and hydrotherapy staff both in the UK and Australia, and all the people who prayed for me and my family. This was as much their journey as mine.

If one person who reads this afterwards:

- goes a little further in their wheelchair or
- takes one step more or
- comes to understand there is God despite all they have gone through, then it has all been worthwhile.

Psalm 139:5
'Thou hast beset me behind and before,
and laid thine hand upon me.'
(KJV)

As a postscript, as I finished my first draft of this story, Joy was diagnosed with a secondary cancer. I am pleased to say that before publication she finds herself in remission. Also, in late-2019 I was able to return to England to scatter my mother's ashes, and attend her well-attended memorial service.

In sport I have been designated a T36 para athlete, which has seen me receiving State medals for 100m, 200m and 400m in the over-50 category. SA Masters Athletics awarded me Best Athlete of the year 2017 and Flinders Athletics, where I am vice president, the Jacob Murray Medal 2017/2018. This was in part for my contribution towards working on a table that sets out to enable disabled athletes to compete against their able-bodied counterparts on a level playing field.

TEN

Living with Deafblindness

by Linda Fistonich and Valerie Everett

THERE IS A SAYING BY THE ANCIENT GREEK PHILOSOPHER, Epictetus, that I hold true to my heart. *It's not what happens to us in life, but how we react to it that matters.* I was diagnosed with a medical condition at an early age, and although faced with many challenges, I responded with personal strength and courage to overcome them.

My name is Linda Fistonich and I was born in Auckland, New Zealand, on 12 June 1962, the youngest of Lucy and Dobrinko Fistonich's four children. My mother thought I was a perfectly normal baby and there was no hint that I would develop optic atrophy, the same congenital eye condition as my brother, Tony. But as time passed, she began to notice that something was wrong.

She knew I could see, but not properly, and the extent of my loss of sight was not known, until it almost ended in tragedy.

One day, my Mum had left me inside the house while she went to the strawberry patch. When she returned, she was shocked to smell smoke. I had thrown a cushion and accidentally knocked over the heater, and although I could smell smoke, I could not clearly see the heater. All I could do was panic, unable to find my way out of the room.

My alarmed parents took me to a specialist, and it was confirmed that I had optic atrophy, which meant the optic nerve was affected, causing my sight to deteriorate. In spite of this, my parents wanted to give me every opportunity possible for a happy childhood. They encouraged me to use the little sight I had and would buy me a book every week to read. We went for long drives and my parents tested my vision but, as time progressed, I could no longer identify objects outside the car.

At the tender age of five, whilst my mum travelled to Yugoslavia (now known as Croatia) with my brother, hoping to find a cure for his sight, my older sister, Sonja, took me to the local primary school. I would be the only blind student there. I enjoyed the school very much because the teacher was kind but, sadly, by the end of the first year, I could no longer read the words on the blackboard.

My parents decided that I would go to Homai College for the Blind in Auckland. I agreed to attend, but if I had known how this school functioned, I would never have gone. It was more like an 'institution' than a school, with strict teachers who expected a lot with little praise. Yet, it was the only school for the blind in New Zealand and the best option for me to be educated as a child with visual loss.

Thankfully, my strict school days at Homai were uplifted by a more joyful side to life. It was during this time that my sister, Katie, took me to see the movie *Funny Girl*, which inspired me to start going to the movies frequently. With my failing sight, I could see the movie if I sat close enough to the screen. Otherwise, I followed the movie by its sound, or listened to my sister's whispered narration of the story, as we sat close in the cinema.

As my sight began to deteriorate further, I faced another challenge. I had to learn how to read and write Braille, which began at the age of eight. My brother, Tony, who was eight years older than me had learned Braille so, naturally, I wanted to be as accomplished as him. It produced a competitive streak in me to succeed, and being the stubborn little girl I was, and the woman I am now, I persisted. I am proud to say that I mastered Braille in just one term at school!

I was very close to Tony and we would listen to quiz games on the radio, the radio soap opera *The Archers*, and many news events. He and I had many similar interests, such as reading and letter writing. When he passed away at the age of nineteen, on 6 May 1973, from suspected pancreatic cancer, I was very shocked and saddened. Even now, many years after his passing, I often think of him and the wonderful times we shared as close siblings.

I had a loving family, but grew up in a Croatian household where, culturally, it was typical for children to be cossetted and supported. Concerned about my medical condition, my parents were naturally anxious about my welfare and over-protective. Consequently, when I was at school, I was not very confident playing with other children in the playground during recess and lunch times. Instead, I preferred to be in the library during breaks. Fortunately, it was in the library that I met Anne Clark, a wonderful deafblind librarian, who became a role model and one of my first great friends. She encouraged my love of reading and to gain knowledge of the world through books, while giving me the confidence to develop myself.

I faced many obstacles at Homai, often caused by other people doubting my capabilities. My blindness, combined with the gradual loss of my hearing, were not always met with understanding by students and teachers, which made my life very difficult. An example of this occurred while learning how to type. I couldn't understand a word in the middle of a sentence on the Dictaphone and when no one told me what the word was, it caused great anxiety. The problem was caused by the fact that I was losing my hearing, not because I was an uncooperative student as the teacher had suggested. This attitude negatively impacted my life and self-esteem for many years to come. I was a capable student, and I did not need criticism or negative reactions, but empathy!

After Homai College, I spent one year at Manurewa Intermediate School, which was close to Homai. The following year, I went to Baradene College, a girls' high school in Auckland, where I was the only blind student in the entire school. My textbooks were given to me in Braille, and I tried to keep up with my peers and the curriculum. Overall, I loved Baradene College because most of the staff and students were so kind and positive towards me. But as integration of a deafblind student into mainstream schooling was still very new, I was unable to receive my text books in Braille on time. As a result, and with no fault of my own, I was usually behind the other students in the learning program. At the end of the year, I was disappointed when I failed my school certificate exams.

Determined to achieve better results, I returned to Manurewa High School. There, my textbooks were easier to access, and I could also attend tutoring after school to catch up on work. At Manurewa, I achieved better grades academically but, sadly, I was teased a lot by other students for being 'prim and proper'. It felt so unfair. At my previous school, I could not keep up with my peers and failed exams. Now, at my new school, I was being teased for my studious attitude!

I also felt some unease on the home front, during my teenage years. My parents continued to be unconditional in their love and support, and I genuinely appreciated how they took such good care of me. Yet, I felt the effects of their over-protection even more. I was aware that other friends were encouraged to be more independent at a younger age than me and I was very isolated, not connecting easily with my peers. My deafblindness added to my perceived helplessness and my parents responded by sheltering me, even more, from the outside world. I did not develop socially like other girls my age. There were no boyfriends in my teenage years, or romances that might lead to marriage and children, or other normal life progressions that other women experience.

I was shy and lacked confidence, but I was determined to succeed with my education. In particular, my will to achieve was sparked at high school, when a teacher commented, 'You are not good enough to go to university!' On Hearing those words, I was determined to prove her wrong and matriculated from Year Twelve.

The following year, I commenced a Bachelor of Psychology at the University of Auckland, part-time, in 1984. I was enjoying my study, but after only two years into the course, my parents decided to leave New Zealand, to make a new life in Perth, Western Australia. So, along with my mum, I flew over just a little after my dad and grandma, as I still had to complete my exams in Auckland University. However my sister Sonja remained living in Auckland. In spite of this, we were grateful to have my other sister, Katie, living in Perth two years beforehand. Because of her help, we settled down and got familiar more quickly than we had expected in our new home.

In 1986, I recommenced my psychology studies at the University of Western Australia, where the staff and students were very helpful in assisting me through the course. Lecturers organised lesson material in Braille, and when I asked for help from my peers, 12-15 fellow students willingly offered. They would visit me and read through their lecture notes which I converted into Braille. These helpful volunteers also did photocopying and read articles to me, which I also transcribed. With this assistance, I had the necessary notes, articles and resources I needed to type up assignments. From my experiences at university, my social life blossomed. I made many friends and was invited to picnics, movies and monthly catch-ups.

Contrary to the doubts of my high school teacher, and other people along the way, I completed my Bachelor in Psychology degree and graduated in 1990. This was one of the highlights of my life. Not only did I prove others wrong, but I also proved to myself that I could achieve anything I set my mind to. Attending university was a positive experience, and I am very proud to have conquered the limitations I faced to achieve my degree.

In 1990, I fulfilled a lifelong dream. It was visiting my relatives in the former Yugoslavia, who I had wanted to visit since I was a little girl. When I first arrived, they too, doubted my capabilities, namely, to travel alone and cope in an overseas country as a deafblind person. But after I had spent some time with them, they were more confident in my abilities. I was very privileged to have gone with my parents in 1990 as I had got to meet my aunts and uncles, who had unfortunately passed soon after my visit. Afterwards, I went to Paris to visit a lifelong deafblind pen pal, who I had been corresponding via tape recordings since 1985.

It was a warm welcome and a rewarding experience to finally meet him. Travelling overseas for that three-month holiday was unforgettable, and the experiences helped me grow significantly in confidence.

On my return to Perth, I overcame yet another challenge as a deafblind person. I secured a position as a telemarketer at *Community Newspapers*, where I ended up working for twenty-two years. Employment demonstrated to my colleagues that, despite my disability, I could work on equal terms alongside them. In turn, they looked beyond my disability and acknowledged my capabilities. They treated me as an equal and, over time, my social interactions with them increased and I formed lifelong friendships. The quote by Robert M Hensel is a true reflection of my experiences at *Community Newspapers*: *"There is no greater disability in society than the inability to see someone as more"*.

Paid employment provided many rewards, but I also wanted to help others. With this goal, I volunteered to help migrants, unemployed individuals, and blind people in Western Australia and across the world. Via email, I offered my friendship and informal counselling, putting what I had learned from my degree in psychology, and own life experiences, to excellent use. In 2012, after many years in this role, I was honoured to be inducted into the Western Australian Women's Hall of Fame in recognition of my commitment to voluntary work.

I was made redundant at *Community Newspapers* in 2012, but within two years, I had broadened my volunteering work. In 2014, I volunteered for Senses Australia, a disability organisation specifically catering for adults and children who are deafblind. While there, a consultant encouraged me to attend a deafblind camp that was to be held in Perth. I was reluctant to go, but after much persuasion, I decided to give it a try and attend. I felt completely out of my comfort zone, but discovered that the camp gave me the opportunity to meet and form friendships with deafblind people, while I participated in recreational activities that were safe and in a supportive environment.

There were many physical challenges while on camp, but I am proud to say that I conquered many, including the flying fox! My positive experiences on the Perth camp encouraged me to attend three additional camps: one in Perth and also Sydney and Melbourne. At every one of the four camps, my life was enriched as I gained confidence, formed friendships and met many inspiring people who won my respect and admiration.

My confidence increased, even more, when I moved into a retirement village on 21 March 2016. Up until my mid-fifties, I was still living a very dependent life with my parents, who carried out most of my daily living tasks. I had everything done for me, from the moment I got up in the morning, until the moment I went to bed at night. All of my decisions were made for me and I had to ask permission to go out, and tell my parents what time I would be coming home. As much as I appreciated my parents' love and how they cared for me, it was a very restricted way of living.

The transition from living with my parents to living on my own was a huge crash course in independence! My older sister, Katie, was invaluable in helping me find the right apartment at Parkland Villas. She also assisted with the necessary paperwork, and the packing and unpacking. Without her, moving out of home would have been impossible.

Once settled in my new home, I needed to develop all of the skills necessary to live independently and socialise with others around me. It was an ongoing learning experience, but I eventually learned to look after myself. With my new freedom, my life in the village has given me a great sense of satisfaction, achievement and the joy of being part of a lively community. I have edited the monthly newsletter, *The Village Voice*, and I regularly attend concerts and other entertainments that are offered.

When I walk around the leafy grounds of the village, which feel safe and secure, everyone is friendly and welcoming. I have wonderful friends and love living here, although there have been a few mishaps along the way. I've had to develop a strategy to exit the building quickly when the fire alarm goes off, plus I occasionally break a glass or knock something over. My bonus, however, is that my power bills are low because I don't need lights!

My life has been an amazing journey. There have been many obstacles and limitations because of my deafblindness, but also many successes. For many years, I wished I could see and hear and that my life would be easier. At the same time, I have met many people who can see and hear, but they have many problems of their own. I believe that life is all about choices and we all face challenges. We could sit in a room isolated from the outside world feeling sorry for ourselves, or we can choose to believe in our abilities. When facing challenges my motto is simple. *Keep taking steps forward, as I have, and I will not look back!* We are all unique individuals and should accept who we are, and not who we wish we could be. I am living proof that challenges can be faced, and one way or another, overcome! I have been on my own journey of fulfilment, from being dependent to independent, from isolation to participating in life as much as possible.

On my life's journey, I have also been willing to accept support from other people. I have been very fortunate to have a family, many friends and work colleagues, who have encouraged me along the way. In particular, I owe a lot to my sister, Katie, who never allowed me to use my blindness and hearing loss to my advantage, or to expect that I should be treated differently. Katie always insisted that I was independent, both physically and emotionally, and that I face the challenges before me. For the encouragement she and others have given me throughout my life, I am truly thankful. With such unconditional support, together with my own determination and courage, I am living a fulfilled life.

If I was asked the question, 'Who am I?' I would answer it like this: I am no longer that little girl who failed to read the words on the blackboard. I am no longer that little girl who was so shy and timid, she hardly said a word in class. Nor am I that little girl who struggled to make friends because of her Croatian background. Rather, I am now a very outgoing, confident and independent woman, who is willing to try new things and step out of my comfort zone. I am proud to be deafblind and have finally accepted this, not as a disability, but as an ability. First and foremost, I am Linda Fistonich.

ELEVEN

A NEWS-Worthy Knock-On

by Jonathan Nguyen and Chantel Bongiovanni

IF YOU WERE TO LOOK AT ME, YOU'D SEE ME AND NOT automatically think 'athlete'.

It's not that anyone is trying to be rude; people just don't always equate an electric wheelchair with competitive sport. Though, it all could have gone quite differently if things didn't fall exactly as they did. Sometimes people can nag and nag at you to do something for years, and you never listen, but a split-second experience can change everything.

That's basically how I wound up in Sydney at the National Electric Wheelchair Sports (NEWS) competition in 2017. It's a week-long national competition (that's been going on since the 80s) for people with neuromuscular conditions who use electric wheelchairs for everyday mobility. Teams compete in three sports: hockey, rugby and balloon soccer. It's quite a sight if you've never seen it, and people are often shocked at the intensity and skill—I don't think even I knew what I was in for! But, I could have very easily not have been in a place like this about to represent South Australia if things had gone differently.

My first introduction to sport happened in primary school. I had always been interested in sport, but being in an electric wheelchair and having decreased physical strength due to my disability, my options for playing sport were basically limited to zilch. I know what you're thinking already, why didn't I play wheelchair basketball? Why didn't I take up murderball? Wheelchair tennis? The truth is, that while those sports work for some, you actually need a fair bit of upper body strength to play them, and that's just not me. I have a form of congenital muscular dystrophy— whichever way you cut it, I just don't have the physical strength for sports like that.

At first look, you'd think I can't play sport. That would be that. My passion for sport was always going to be just an *outside looking in* type of passion. A passion I could have, but do nothing with.

However, the thing that everyone seems to forget is, is that there's *always* someone, somewhere, pushing the envelope on what's possible.

Fortunately, knocking on the doors of my destiny were some mates with disabilities at my school who played in local competitions. My friend Sam would often try to talk me into it: 'Come out, we need you!' he'd say. Now, it might not seem that odd for my friends at school to try to get me to play a sport, but this was also the only choice they had in trying to find new players. Electric wheelchair sports like mine are notoriously unheard of: 'What? You play basketball?' (If only I had a dollar for every time I've been asked that question). Unless it's by word of mouth, people just don't realise you can play sport in an electric wheelchair. Heck, there's nothing stopping you from playing sport—that's what I learnt later on. If you have a way to move the controller on your chair, you can play sport. But people just don't know. I didn't know. So that's how I came to be there, twelve years old, and being recruited to sport by my school friends.

Mind you, I didn't start out as a protégé or as a wheelchair-playing prodigy; my beginnings were far humbler than that. I played with my mates Trav and Sam throughout primary school rather than joining any official junior group. Because of our respective disabilities, the school found it hard to include us in PE with the other kids. Instead, they grouped us together. We mostly played a version of balloon soccer. I later found out, when I joined a more organised competition, that this was a version with very loose rules where basically anything went. We kicked with our feet, sometimes we used our hands, or we head-butted the ball. There were no rules, and I liked the freedom to play as I wanted.

It wasn't until I was thirteen and in my first year of high school when I went to join the official competition, finally. I was a bundle of nerves that night. Mum drove me and we got lost on the way. The playing hall was behind a school; it was after-hours, and we wandered around the school for a while trying to find our way—Mum thought we were gonna get robbed, but we survived!

Once we found the entrance to the gym and got inside, I didn't know who to talk to; I didn't know where to begin. Soon, I realised I was early, no one I knew had arrived yet, and I was shy and unsure. Bear in mind, I was only thirteen, and this was an entirely new world for me. Someone eventually saw my nervousness. He introduced himself as one of the team captains, and before I knew where I was—I was playing. I actually don't remember much of the games themselves that night. I was on such a high just to be there. The games were more fast-paced than I had imagined and I quickly discovered how rudimentary my understanding of the games was. But for me, it was exhilarating just to play against my friends from school in a competitive setting. It was so much fun; I'd never imagined I'd do something like this.

After that, I was hooked. I had to keep playing.

But, it wasn't always simple to actually get to play my games. At first, we had a wheelchair-accessible van, and my mum would drive me to sport. However, tragically, the van was stolen one day while my mum was out. It was later found dumped in the middle of a lake. My family couldn't afford a new van. After that, I had to rely on taxis or lifts from friends. I guess you do what you gotta do, right? It wasn't easy though, I'll admit that. Our playing season was also held during the winter months back then, and I was susceptible to getting sick a lot. Sometimes it took a lot of work to convince my mum to let me go to sport if there was bad weather about, as she didn't want me getting sick. The odds were against me, and it was only my dedication and willingness to keep playing that kept me coming out. I wanted to keep playing and I was quite determined to continue.

Even though there was a national competition, I played in local teams for ten years—from my teens into my early twenties, but I *never* tried out for the state team.

There were many reasons. One of them was that I had never left South Australia before. I'd never even been on a plane, and the majority of the time, our competitions happened in Sydney. My mum was scared about how I'd cope traveling on a plane because of my disability. Alongside muscular dystrophy, I have restrictive lung disease. When I was young, doctors told mum that it was risky to let me travel because of my breathing, and she had stuck to that into my adulthood. Really, we'd just avoided the issue of me travelling by not travelling at all. But that was changing, and I didn't want it to always be this way. Not only had I been playing for a long time, but I'd see my friends try out and travel year-to-year for competitions. Like when I was kid, they'd come up to me and give me this gentle clip behind the ears. Instead of my mate Sam asking, 'Why don't you play sport?' it had become 'Jono, are you gonna come to NEWS this year? Jono, you'd be good if you came with us.' Truthfully, it wore me down. I played with them, I trained with them, but I never travelled to competitions with them.

In more recent years, our local league had been struggling for numbers, and this trend had filtered to our state team – we simply did not have enough new players joining our local teams. As a community-based, unfunded group, we had to work really hard to try to get new potential players involved. This struggle resonated with me. Year by year, week after week, I was starting to come around to the idea of travelling to play, because I knew I could do my part if I had the chance; even if I didn't say anything to anyone. There was the issue of flying by plane and convincing my mum I could fly (I ended up taking a lung function test so a doctor could assure her it was safe for me to travel). I also needed to find someone to support me while I was there, as I need support and help with daily tasks. But despite all that, the thing that held me back was more than that: I think I just didn't have the courage to make that final leap.

In life, sometimes the push to take that final leap can take many forms. In my case, it would be a knock to the head.

It started out like any other normal game. It was balloon soccer. I was playing 'six' (that's a position where I do the majority of the ball control to defend and attack). At first, nothing was amiss. It was a tight game. Both sides were jostling and playing hard for the ball. The opposition's six took a hit-in from the side, and I rushed forward to cut off his run. I must have clipped someone's chair, and my wheel rolled up over a footplate or bull bar (that's a metal bar attached to the front of the chair that protects your feet while you're playing). All I knew was that I was in the air, going sideways. I remember those split seconds so vividly. Time slowed; the world around me seemed to be more drawn out as a became aware that I was hanging in mid-air. There was a powerlessness to it; I couldn't stop what was about to happen.

Everything went black.

When I came to, I was lying on the ground, and I was not in my wheelchair any more. There were people all around me, and everyone seemed overly-concerned. I wanted to say, 'I'm fine', but obviously if I was on the floor, something had gone wrong. I heard one of my teammates say, 'He's got that no one's home look in his eyes'. I didn't understand what he meant at the time.

My head.

Everything was foggy.

At some point, someone found a pillow and put it under my head. I lay there trying to sort out where I was and what had happened.

In the end, once we were sure there was no great damage, some of the parents of the other players helped me slowly back into my chair. They called an ambulance just in case, and I got checked at the hospital. Light concussion, sore collarbone, and no major damage. I was discharged and cleared to go home that night. That was my first major fall in a decade of playing, and though I wasn't hurt, it lit a fire in me.

What if it happens again? What if I can't play? What if I stopped playing and I never did all the things I could do? What if I could have done more? These thoughts plagued me. I didn't want my time to be up without giving it all I had. I couldn't do it anymore. I didn't want to just listen to everyone else's stories of going interstate to play, of their victories and their defeats. I wanted my own story.

So I signed up. I tried out. I made that leap.

Finally.

I found a support worker, who had known me since high school, to support me while I was away. It was important to find someone my mum knew to ease her apprehension. This was my first time on a plane, my first time leaving Adelaide, ever. Everything was a blur in Sydney; there was so much to take in, and I was overwhelmed. I had seen online videos of the stadium we were playing in before, and it looked small then. In person, it was huge. Everything I had seen and heard appeared bigger in the flesh. Maybe because it was real now. It was tangible, and I was here, finally living something that had been a decade in the making.

Game day arrived quickly. As I put my number on, I was all nerves. I ran over plays in my head: *What did I need to do? What if I couldn't? What if this was wrong?* I thought back to all the moments that had led me here. The insecurity. The uncertainty. Mum still wasn't sure about me travelling. Even as I left Adelaide, she still wasn't entirely convinced.

The siren sounded.

We were up. It was time. I pushed all thoughts of doubt to the back of my mind and headed out onto the court.

I'd like to think I was prepared for my first game. That's what I told myself– I was ready. I was ready to play against Western Australia. But my nerves got me right off the bat. In rugby league, there's no margin for error when it comes to holding the defensive line, because your errors reverberate and impact throughout the line. I made a miscalculation, and before I could even correct myself, a Western Australian player was through for a try. I tried to reset, to forget it and move on. I was tentative and tense. I continued in attack; six tackles came around quickly, and we were on the defensive again. I tried to hold my place in the line this next time around. I didn't want to let another try through. By this point I knew they were zoning in on my area in the defensive line because I was a rookie, because they saw me as having the least experience, because I presented myself as a weak link in our team for them to exploit.

The player with the ball came up in my area and I went to tackle him, but he made a quick pass to the guy next to him. There was a gap, he was gonna get through, there was gonna be another try. In the moment, I tried to backtrack and reversed to cut off his run before he broke the line. The whistle blew and the umpire approached. I knew what I'd done as the whistle blew. The umpire gave me a warning. Reverse tackling is outlawed as dangerous play because there's a risk of damaging the opposing player's chair or worse, injuring the attacking player. It's easy to forget in the moment and reverse tackle when you're not thinking straight, because at that point instincts kick in. I cringed and berated myself, but I was trying to maintain my outward composure. On the inside, I was a raging storm of nerves and I was trying to keep it buried down in my gut. I was a spring coiled so tightly, I was gonna spring at any second ... and we were still in our first half!

The next moment, I heard our coach, Scott, on the sidelines trying to get my head back on straight. He could tell I was struggling. 'Don't worry about it, Nguyen,' he said between the plays, 'don't be overawed by them! Keep it simple, keep your position on the defensive line!'

I took a deep breath and tried to focus. *I can do this*. The game began to flow. I calmed down and focused on what was in front of me. I held my line. I even managed to score a try which went a long way towards settling my nerves. The siren sounded. We won.

I let out a sigh of relief that I didn't realise I'd been holding in that whole time.

I picked up the speed of the competition after that game, as I became more confident. Yeah, the games were way faster and competitive than anything I'd done before, but I adapted a lot quicker than I thought I would. I held myself together. Soon, the other teams knew I wasn't an easy target any more.

We battled on throughout the week. I held my ground; I grew surer in my teammates and they grew surer in me. Playing sport in a competition like that happens fast. The days are long. Filled not just with playing, but team meetings and planning. Before I knew it, we were in the finals. I don't think I was prepared for the elation.

South Australia competed in one of its most successful years at NEWS in over twenty years. It was borderline shocking; it was emotional. We were champions in balloon soccer for the first time since 1994, and were runners-up in rugby and hockey. We were awarded the Roger Melnyk Trophy – a trophy designated for the most dominating team of the round-robin. South Australia hadn't won a *Roger* (as it's more affectionately known) since 1992. As a team, we were the worst winners. We literally celebrated until well after everyone had become bored and left the stadium, and even then, we were still going. We were elated and unapologetic about our happiness. The win had an impact on me that I never anticipated. I kept seeing how much had changed for me, that the impossibility had become a possibility and had opened up so many doors for me – I wanted more people to have that.

I went home more motivated than I ever had been before. I wanted to play more, than was definite and I immediately signed up for more interstate competitions. After being there, after competing like that, I understood why opportunities for sport needed to happen for people with disabilities. It wasn't just winning a game. It wasn't only about developing new skills. It was the camaraderie between my teammates and my interstate peers. It was discovering I could do something I never thought I would do and succeeding at that. I just didn't want that to disappear for those that came after me; losing that would be a huge loss.

Back in Adelaide, I volunteer every week in a junior sports league for children with disabilities aged five to fourteen. I teach them to play; I try to motivate them to see the opportunities they have with sport. It doesn't really matter what they can or can't do, it's about understanding that there's always an option, even if you can't directly see it. There's always a way forward, and there's always something you can do, even if you need a knock to the head to realise it.

TWELVE

Will You Die Before Your Death?

by Tracey Meg and May-Kuan Lim

A SMALL ORANGE FLAG FLUTTERS FROM A POLE ATTACHED TO the back of Tracey's[9] wheelchair. She is going to participate in an interview with her favourite Minions, Stuart, Bob and Kevin, characters from the movie, *Despicable Me*. No one understands Minion gibberish? Not to worry, it's been translated for you.

Kevin: Thank you for coming into the studio, Tracey.
Tracey: It's a pleasure to be here.
Bob: Who brought you here?
Tracey: I brought myself here.

---

9   Not her real name

Bob: But you can't move your legs. You can barely move your hands. Surely someone helped you to get from your house across town to our studio?

Tracey: No, no, no. I travelled from my house to the bus stop in my powered wheelchair. The bus driver got out of his seat and flipped out the ramp so that I could drive my wheelchair up onto the bus. I only needed help when I got here, remember?

Kevin: Sorry about that. Stuart is forever leaving boxes by the entrance ...

Stuart: That's how I remind myself to take them home later.

Tracey: You made the doorway too narrow for me, Stuart. Designers nowadays use universal access design principles to build or modify roads and buildings or even websites that are accessible to all. But their work is undone by stuff left in doorways or cars parked across walkways. It makes it really hard, or sometimes impossible, for people like me to get around.

Stuart: But there are not many people like you, are there, Tracey?

Tracey: Well, maybe not people exactly like me, but have you noticed older people in scooters? Or people on crutches because they broke or temporarily injured their leg? Or people with visual impairment using a white cane? They could easily trip over an obstacle and have a bad fall. A little lack of consideration can cause big trouble.

Kevin: And with medical advances enabling people to live longer, I suppose enabling older people to get around independently will become increasingly important.

Tracey: Yes, and remember that small kindnesses can go a long way. Sometimes, when going to a restaurant with manually-operated doors or few steps, I have to wait to see if anyone will offer to open the door for me or any other entrance without steps.

I once waited for fifteen minutes just for someone to come out so that I could go in. I suggested to the manager that he add a wireless doorbell or purchase a portable ramp. Surely it's not too difficult to make such small changes?

Bob: Luckily you have plenty of spare time, Tracey.

Tracey: You know, Bob, I'm very busy. I have a busy social life. I love organising parties for my friends and relatives—Chinese New Year parties, facial parties, waffle parties. I manage all my own appointments—physiotherapy, pedicure, sailing …

Stuart: Sailing? You couldn't go sailing!

Tracey: Stuart, if you keep up this negative talk, I'm going to leave. I don't have time for people who put me down.

Kevin *(kicking Stuart under the table):* Stuart is sorry. Tracey, tell us about your sailing.

Tracey: I have always loved being outdoors and am a very active person. I first learnt how to sail in Hong Kong before my accident. Back then, I ran mini-marathons, learnt paragliding, and even sailed from Hong Kong to Shenzhen in a regatta.

Bob: Where is Shenzhen?

Tracey: In south-east China.

Bob: Whoa! How long did that take?

Tracey: At least six hours.

Bob: You must have been very tired.

Tracey: Well, I was part of a team, and we all had our part to play, so it wasn't too bad. But you're right, that was too long for me. I preferred short sailing trips around Hong Kong itself. While I was in Hong Kong, I heard about 'Sailability', but then forgot about it.

Bob: What's Sailability?

Tracey: It's an international organisation where volunteers take people for short sailing trips. After my injury in 2013, I heard there was Sailability in Adelaide. 'Oh! This is very good', I said to myself. 'They pair you with an experienced volunteer who can control the boat. I won't be in the boat by myself. I won't need to do all the setup and boat handling! Since the volunteers cater to each person's ability, I can choose to control the boat with my left hand (which is stronger), or just enjoy the breeze and the interplay of wind, water and boat. The boat is safe too—it has been tested and will not turn over even if it is full of water. I've been sailing with Sailability for about three years now. During the sailing season, when the weather is good, I sail about once a month.

Bob: When you say that you go sailing, do you really mean that you sit in a wheelchair in the sailboat?

Tracey: No, no, no. My wheelchair cannot fit on the boat. Sailability uses small boats that can fit two people only. So when I go sailing, I travel in my wheelchair to a hoist that is fixed to the jetty. Sailability volunteers put a sling around my body, and winch me up using the hoist. They then lower me into the sailboat. They always put me on the right side of the boat so that my left hand, which is stronger, can move the controls and control the rudder.

Kevin: Tracey, you mentioned your accident. Can you tell us a bit about that?

Tracey: In 2013, I was travelling in the Northern Territory, on a working holiday visa, when I was involved in a horrific motor vehicle accident and suffered a C5 level of injury.

Bob: Injuries get report cards? Like at school—A, B, C, D?

Tracey: No, Bob. C5 refers to the bone in my neck where my spinal cord was injured. As a result of my spinal cord injury, or SCI for short, I could not move my body from my chest down and became tetraplegic. This means that all four of my limbs were affected by some degree of paralysis.

Kevin: What has been the biggest challenge for you since your accident?

Tracey: The two biggest challenges for me now are life-threatening situations and finding reliable support workers.

Stuart: Life-threatening situations—a bit dramatic, don't you think, Tracey? Apart from your limited mobility, you look as if you're in pretty good health.

Tracey: SCI doesn't just limit my mobility. The spinal cord is like a two-way communication link. Before my accident, my brain could send instructions to the rest of my body via my spinal cord. Nerves in my body also sent information back to my brain via the spinal cord; for example: *am I hot or cold? is there pain? is there discomfort?* But since the injury, this communication link has been affected. As a result, I have trouble regulating my blood pressure and body temperature. Limited mobility makes me more susceptible to skin sores, and there is also the very serious AD.

Bob: What is AD?

Kevin: It stands for 'Autonomic Dysreflexia', which is when the body remains on high alert to counter some sort of discomfort, such as a full bladder. Because of Tracey's spinal cord injury, her body does not receive the signal to relax from her brain. Therefore, her body remains in a prolonged state of high alert.

Tracey: The first time I experienced AD was just a few weeks before being discharged from the rehabilitation centre. My heart was racing super-fast. I could barely breathe. I was sweating and had a terrible headache. I thought I was going to die.

Bob: But you didn't die. Obviously.

Tracey: No, the doctors intervened. But it was very scary for me. It's been five years since my injury and these days I don't get AD too often when my bladder is super full. Leaking is a more of a problem as my muscle slackens and the liquid finds another pathway to escape.

Bob: Why don't you just go to the toilet?

Tracey: Because of SCI, I cannot hold my pee in, and this is very inconvenient. So doctors have connected a tube—or a catheter—that goes through a hole near my belly button into my bladder. At other end of the catheter is a leg-bag to hold the urine. But it's not a foolproof system. Once, my carer did not connect it up properly and I had to lie in a urine pool, being marinated overnight. The next morning, my bum, my back and my legs were wet, and I was smelly. I joked with my carer, 'Do you like creating work? A little clip not opened at night, and in the morning you need to wipe me, clean me, and shower me.' Between AD and leaking, I prefer leaking as my life is not in immediate danger, but my skin may deteriorate. If there is broken skin, I could get an infection. This happened towards the end of 2014 when I had plastic surgery, not for my face or my breast, but for my bum and back in 2015. Haha!

Stuart: Poor Tracey.

Tracey: Don't pity me. I don't like pity.

Stuart: What I mean is that I feel sorry for you.

Bob: Because so many bad things could happen to you.

Tracey: Bad things can happen to any of us. Life is fragile, but it's true that life with SCI is even more fragile. Apart from low blood pressure, I can easily suffer heat stroke because my body thermostat has been disconnected. On very hot days, my body temperature can rise very quickly. Even though my limbs may be very warm, I will not sweat. If I am in danger of heat stroke, I will feel my heart beating very fast, headache, have difficulty breathing and become very tired. Even if I sit in front of an air conditioner, these symptoms can persist.

Bob: Is there anything you can do?

Tracey: I need to drink plenty of water, and wipe my limbs, forehead, face and neck with a cold, damp cloth. So, if I plan to go out, even if it is only for a short fifteen minutes, I will always check the weather forecast beforehand and cancel my trip if the temperature is over thirty-five degrees.

Bob: So cold days are better for you?

Tracey: Not really. In cold weather, I wear thermal vests to contain my body heat. I wear fleece and down jackets as insulators, and even a ski jacket to stop the wind. Most important is to keep my head warm under a beanie, and my feet warm in socks and UGG boots or minion slippers.

Stuart: Minion slippers look much nicer than Ugg boots, but even so, it just seems like so much effort, for a simple task. If I were you, I would just stay at home. It's probably safer for someone like you to stay at home anyway.

Tracey: If I do that I will be dying before my time. I didn't die in the car accident, but my first life was over. I think of my life after my injury as my second life. It's a second chance to see new things, experience new things. Bob let me ask you, have you been to the Alberton Oval?

Bob: Yeah, I've been there to watch Port Power play.

Tracey: How about the Old Gaol Museum where prisoners stayed in the old days?

Bob: No.

Tracey: Have you watched the raced model yachts in Mawson Lakes?

Bob: No.

Tracey: Have you been to the Adelaide Planetarium to see the projection of stars and the universe?

Bob: No.

Tracey: Well, Bob, you are able-bodied and I'm not, but I have been to so many places you have not been to.

Bob: That's true, Tracey. How about you take me along sometime?

Tracey: I'll have to ask Mick from PQSA.

Bob: PQSA?

Kevin: Paraquad South Australia – PQSA.

Tracey: Usually it's for people who are in wheelchairs. There are around fifteen of us, all in wheelchairs, and Mick organises these trips for us fortnightly.

Bob: Must cost a lot of money to go on so many trips.

Tracey: Not really. I take public transport to most of the outings under PQSA's Recreation Program, which is usually free, or a small ticket fee involved. Then I might spend a few dollars for a cup of coffee and a cake at a café after to catch up with my friends. But I must say that after visiting the Planetarium, I enrolled in a Stars and Planets Course by run by the University of South Australia that cost a bit of money.

Stuart: What? You paid money to attend lectures? Are you a sucker for suffering?

Tracey: No, I'm a curious person who loves learning. I've wanted to study planets and stars since I was young but had no time.

Bob: From the highest heavens to the depths of the sea—what are you going to say next, Tracey, that you go scuba diving?

Tracey: Yes, in fact I do, but not in the sea. Not yet, only at the aquatic centre in North Adelaide. There's this guy, Peter; he had a motorcycle accident, and had all this rehab, but they didn't fix the bad thoughts going through his mind like low self-esteem and negativity. So he founded Determined2.

Bob: Determined to? To what? Sounds like half a name.

Tracey: To recover, to improve, it's up to the people with injury or disability to decide what they are determined to do. Peter and his team help them by using 'Immersion Therapy'. It's not just physical therapy, but it's giving people back the agency to decide how they want to proceed with their therapy.

Stuart: Don't give me the marketing talk, Tracey. Tell me what they do.

Tracey: They winch me out of my wheelchair into the water, help me get an oxygen mask over my face, an oxygen tank on my back and whee! I'm free to move in the water. I love the feeling of submerging my whole self into the water. I don't have to listen to noise or talk to people. I'm in a world of my own.

Kevin: Tracey, what you're telling us is amazing. Is there anything you cannot do?

Tracey: Although I can do many things, but I am often dependent on others. For example, I could not go for Immersion Therapy until I found a suitable carer to meet me at the aquatic centre to help me change into my swimming suit. But one time, my carer slept in, so I had to cancel my session. I decided not to book her in for my Immersion Therapy any more. To me, the most important trait in a carer is reliability. Unreliable carers cancel for all sorts of reasons: too tired from having worked an overnight shift or a double shift, having assignments due, or another job, having a most unprofessional attitude to their job, as if it were a playdate, cancelled on a whim.

Kevin: What other characteristics do you look for in a carer?

Tracey: Having professional standards of hygiene, be alert and respect privacy. Treating me with respect - my hands may grip like a baby's hands, but I am not a baby, so don't treat me like one. Availability. Once I asked for emergency help, but nobody came. I hope for a carer who cares, not just about the pay, but for my wellbeing. The reality of my second life is that I must rely on others for help.

Bob: Must be very hard for you.

Tracey: Actually, in the months after my injury, I was even more reliant on others. I could not move my fingers at all. I could not pick up objects around me, except by trying to use both my arms as forceps.

Bob: Like two long chopsticks.

Tracey: Yeah, the chopsticks were too long so I would not have even been able to feed myself if not for the creativity of the OT.

Bob: OT?

Tracey: Occupational Therapists. They gave me a 'Palmer Pocket'. This is a strap around my palm, with a pocket on the strap. They put a spoon or fork into the pocket, and I learnt to feed myself; new problems need new solution — very creative.

Bob: So this palmer pocket helped you to be independent?

Tracey: No, palmer pocket was only used for me to feed myself. For everything else, I still needed a support worker with me all the time. I am like a busy bee, you see; I'm not like people who might sit quietly all day. I was still trying to do many things and was constantly asking for help. I disliked saying 'please' and 'thank you' over and over again because I saw how bored and annoyed my support workers were, as if they were voice-controlled robots or slaves, as if I were wasting their time. It reminded me of the song 'Issues' by Julia Michaels: '... Yeah, I've got issues, and one of them is how bad I need you...'

Kevin: But now you are here in our studio all by yourself, no support worker. What happened?

Tracey: I had two nerve and tendon operations, one in April 2014 and another in April 2016. After prolonged postoperative rehabilitation, I regained the use of my fingers in my left hand.

Like babies learning how to use their hands, I can grip and release objects, even though my fingers cannot open and close individually. My life has become so much better. Now I can cut paper using modified scissors, turn on the tap using a modified tool to push or pull the tap lever, and press an electronic button to open my entrance door. Although I still cannot lift objects that are too small or too big, too slippery or too heavy, I can pay for things using cash or coins, hold an ice cream, and swipe and type on my tablet phone. My tablet has become my home office hub. Thank God for technology - even though it can sometimes fail. On a recent trip to Kangaroo Island, my portable hoist broke down. Luckily a friend could lift me out of my wheelchair or bed. Otherwise I would have been stuck in my wheelchair for three days and two nights.

Kevin: The fanciest technology that doesn't work is of no use to anyone.

Bob: But when it works it's super-cool. I saw a TV commercial on voice-activated home automation. Then your lights can be on or off!

Tracey: Yeah, that'll be good. At the moment, I need help to get a drink from the fridge, but I can hold it myself, using my insulated cup.

[Tracey extracts a big blue plastic cup from one of the numerous bags hanging from her wheelchair and holds it up.]

Bob: Wow, your cup is huge!

[Bob grabs the cup, and pours some lemonade into it and offers it to Tracey, smiling.]

Bob: Thirsty, Tracey?

Tracey (annoyed): No, I am not thirsty. I was just showing you what my cup looks like.

Bob: No need to get upset, Tracey. I was trying to be Tracey-friendly. I was trying to help.

Tracey: It is very important that you ask before you help. Don't assume that I want this or I want that. I have spinal cord injury, not brain injury.

Bob: Shall I pour the drink away, and dry your cup for you?

Tracey: Yes, and put it back inside this bag on my left, the blue stripy bag.

[Bob does as she says.]

Tracey: It's good that you want to help, Bob. But remember to ask first, 'Do you need help?' or 'Are you OK?' Ask sincerely and check first what people's preferences are. I am a self-oriented lady, I will ask for help when I need. I always say that my possessions are my treasure, and my room is my 'Traceytory'.

Bob: Sounding a bit Traceytorial. Hahaha, Tracey is Traceytorial – get it?

Tracey: Bob, try to understand. I have several different carers and they must put things back where they found them otherwise we will be having treasure hunt every day.

Kevin: Sounds like half your challenge is managing physical limitations, and the other half is managing people.

Tracey: What you say is very true. There are all sorts of people in this world. Once there was a naughty boy who came up to me and started fiddling with my wheelchair. His parents were there, and they didn't stop him. If children are curious about my wheelchair, I don't mind showing them the controls and even letting them press some buttons, but they must ask politely first.

Kevin: Children can be awkward—they are just so honest and don't always know how to treat others respectfully.

Tracey: Adults can be worse. Once, at the gym, a few staff members gave me a hard time by overriding the controls on my wheelchair. I was so angry. I said that I would report them to their manager if they did that again.

Bob: Your wheelchair controls can be overridden? Where?

Tracey: I've since had those controls taken out.

Kevin: Do you find that people who don't know you as a person give you the hardest time?

Tracey: Yes and no. Some parents are quick to move their children away from me when they see me approaching. They make me feel as if I am a monster. But some people who knew me before my accident still cannot accept that what happened to me four years ago was an accident. They want me to say, 'It's my mistake' or 'It's my fault for going travelling'. Such talk is like the black holes I learnt about in my Stars and Planet talk. Black holes suck all light from their surrounds. I can't control how people think or what they say, but if anyone talks like that to me, I will run far, far away so that I will not be sucked into their black hole.

Stuart: Maybe it's because those people love you and wish you had all the freedom and functionality of an able body as you had before your accident.

Tracey: Do you know, Stuart, that before my accident, I often felt that my life was meaningless? Now every day I'm experiencing new things and learning new things. I consider this my second life. I feel like a newborn baby learning to live again. Since young, I have been a very independent person. I believe that everything depends on me and I depend on God.

Stuart: God? I would have thought that your accident either proves that there is no God, or, if there is a God, he either doesn't love you enough or isn't powerful enough to give you a miracle healing.

Tracey: In my Stars and Planet course, my lecturer taught me about the great telescopes.

Stuart: Phew! I thought you were getting all religious on me, that you were going to talk about the great God, but you talk about great telescopes instead.

Tracey: Just listen, Stuart, won't you? With our naked eye, we can observe light in the visible wavelength spectrum. But there is also light in the invisible wavelength spectrum, such as microwaves, infrared, x-ray. Great telescopes collect information in the invisible wavelength spectrum. Things happen beyond our visual sphere. We are only human, not super-human, and become easily discouraged if we focus our eyes on our problems. I have learnt to look at the heavenly reality. God may not remove the situation we face, but God knows and provides what we need as He is Love, Grace and Powerful.

Bob: What do you mean by heavenly reality? Sounds like an oxymoron.

Tracey: I am now in heaven as God's love and grace are with me and enough for me to face different situations. God has provided angels around me. These angels provide support and assistance, time and energy to allow me to experience so many things. Will I die before my death? Without them, my heart, mind and soul would have died long ago. In addition, I have learnt to exercise creativity to solve new problems, apply resilience to face adversity and remember my reliance on God every day. I consider my life is flourishing and thriving.

Kevin: Indeed it is. Tracey, it's been great getting to know you. How can our listeners keep up with your adventures?

Tracey: Easy. Follow my blog at welcometomyqueendom.com. It's been great to talk to you, too, Kevin, Bob and Stuart. Who would have thought that Minions were so articulate and a woman on a wheelchair so adventurous?

THIRTEEN

What We're Wheelie Like
by Gail Miller

IF I WANDER UP AND DOWN AND TURN AROUND SO YOU CAN SEE me from all angles, it's impossible for anyone to identify my disability/disorder. According to the audiences to whom I've spoken, I have a knee issue, a neck problem or a dickie hip. Thankfully, none of these afflictions ail me.

What I *do* have is Type 1 diabetes, and I use an insulin pump that keeps me in good health.

It puzzles me that no one treats me like an exception, an oddity or a freak, yet I have a disorder that I've carried around for twenty-seven years, and that will remain with me until I vacate the planet.

Why then did my mum, who walked with an artificial leg, suddenly morph into a person worthy of incredible interest whenever we took her out in a wheelchair?

The seed of an idea for a book began many years ago. Let me take you back to when I was seventeen.

―

I grew up in a happy family of five, with Mum and Dad, an older sister and a younger brother. Picture Mum and Dad's excitement, as they packed their green, Ford Fairmont sedan, with caravan hitched behind, ready to embark on their first holiday without the children. My sister was twenty, and we were old enough to look after ourselves, so off they went, caravanning through New South Wales.

It was early June 1974, on a Tuesday evening, when I was home alone. The door knocker fell heavily against our wooden front door. As I gingerly opened the door and looked out into the dark night, my eyes met those of the kind and gentle, slightly balding minister from our church.

My stomach churned, as this was a most unusual time for him to be visiting. *What could this mean?* I wondered.

'Please come in Mr Anderson,' I said and motioned for him to sit on the lounge.

If you'd been in the lounge on that wintery night, you'd have heard him say in a quiet and deliberate voice, 'I'm sorry to tell you Gail, but your parents were involved in a serious car accident today. They're alright—sort of. Your mum has a serious, but not life-threatening injury and has been taken to the Dubbo Base Hospital,' he said.

'Your dad asked if I would break the news to you, as he knew that it would be impossible for him to fight his way through the tears over the phone, if he tried to tell you himself,' he continued.

Dubbo lies on an expansive plain in central NSW, intersected by a seemingly-endless highway, with Tomingley Bridge, bang smack in the middle of twenty miles of perfectly straight road.

If you'd been in the passenger seat of their car, where Mum sat, you'd have felt the massive jolt from behind, as a huge refrigerated semi-trailer hit the top back corner of Mum and Dad's caravan. The car and caravan jack-knifed, which sent the van careering recklessly over the embankment and into the creek below.

You'd also have felt, as Mum did, the thunderous crash as *her* side of the car, level with the dashboard, met with the huge, unmoving, concrete pylon at the start of the bridge, sending the engine flailing into the creek-bed to their right.

Imagine their terror, as they flew along the bridge at such a speed, that all the concrete posts appeared to be a picket fence. Sitting stationary after an event that was over in seconds, Mum saw that her door was missing, and her legs were somewhere beneath the car—or at least one of them was.

Mum, cool as a cucumber, looked down and said to Dad, 'My leg's gone. Can you run back to the caravan and get a towel to make a tourniquet for what's left?'

Due to the frequency of the accidents on that perilous stretch of road, the local Rotarians had formed a group named the Highway Samaritans and what an appropriate name! They truly were Mum and Dad's Good Samaritans.

They were on the accident scene almost immediately to impound the car when given police clearance; they looked after the valuables, provided accommodation for Dad and transport to the hospital and several became life-long friends to my parents.

What a wonderful service of kindness these people bring!

Back in 1974, seatbelts weren't compulsory, but Mum and Dad always wore them outside the metropolitan area, because they felt safer. Picture the scene: had they *not* been wearing them—or perhaps don't. It may have been a very different result.

Dubbo Hospital was Mum's home for a time, then she was airlifted back to Adelaide, where she recovered in the Royal Adelaide Hospital.

Do you remember watching children learn to walk? Have you any idea how nerve-wracking it was for us to watch our mum, a grown adult, learn to walk, with her thigh suctioned into a fibreglass-like thigh, to which a strange pole with a foot was attached? That was her first artificial leg.

I never heard her complain. She did her exercises and walking practice, went to lots of appointments, looked after us again when she'd recovered enough, started driving again, as soon as she could, but she *never complained*.

Mum could have become outrageously angry about her disability. She could have ranted and raved about the injustice of it all. Instead, she *pressed on regardless.* She said to me one day, 'I should have died in the accident, but I didn't. I guess God isn't finished with me yet.'

One year when we had a hard rubbish collection, Dad came in from the shed holding two artificial legs. 'Can we get rid of these?' he asked Mum. They need to be replaced over time, so you accumulate spares that are of no use to anyone. 'Of course you can', Mum said, 'but don't just plonk them on the footpath. Why don't you droop them over the old television that's on our rubbish pile? That would be funny.'

Picture the scene—two rubbish collectors *not* leaping out of their truck. Can you imagine their faces, the uncertainty in their eyes, as they tentatively approached the body, slumped limply over the TV?

Their trepidation was quickly replaced with great amusement, so they devised a plan that would humour them for the day. All the other rubbish went into their truck, but not the legs. Compactor trucks were still a futuristic concept, so they were in their old-fashioned tip truck. They drooped one leg over the right back corner and the other to the far left and with an ear-to-ear grin on each face, they drove off. 'How good is a sense of humour?'

One of Mum's great pleasures was to go to the Royal Adelaide Show. My grandparents had life membership of the Show Society, so, as a child, during Show Week, it was Mum's second home. She knew every nook and cranny of the showground, but as she couldn't walk long distances with her artificial leg, I took her in a wheelchair.

At the handicraft section, Mum hopped out of the chair to have a closer look at the exhibits, and I sat in the wheelchair for a rest. This was a very educational half-hour of wheelchair respite.

'Hello dear,' some said in a slow, deliberate voice, whilst staring me in the eye and about six inches from my face. Talk about invasion of personal space! Others stared like I was a total oddity; a third group spoke to me in a babyishly demeaning voice; and the last group shouted at me like I was totally deaf.

Why was it that the wheelchair had robbed me of the abilities that I'd possessed just a few minutes prior? I realised that people had made the assumption that because I was in a wheelchair, I must be cognitively impaired.

Mum eventually came back, and we headed back outside into the crowds. 'Mum,' I asked, 'Do people treat you any differently when I take you out in the wheelchair?' 'Yes. All the time. It's like my brain is not connected, the moment I sit in the chair and yet everyone treats me like a regular person when I'm walking. Odd, isn't it?'

That thought lurked in the deep recesses of my brain for thirty-five years. In her mid-seventies Mum became a paraplegic after she had thirteen hours of aortic bypass surgery, with paralysis as a known risk. So, then she spent every day in a wheelchair and had a whole extra set of issues to contend with. I guessed that if Mum had issues, so did other wheelchair users.

I'd thought of writing a book, *but how do I start?* I wondered. *I'm fifty-five and too old to write a book anyway and I don't know how*, I convinced myself.

Around that time, I went to a breakfast at which Margo Bates was speaking. She was an Adelaide woman, with silver hair and beautiful soft wrinkly skin that many elderly people have. Margo was ninety-nine years old when we met and beneath that gentle exterior hid a feisty, determined spirit.

After watching a friend's granddaughter at her swimming lesson one day, Margo approached the instructor and asked, 'Can you teach me to do that?'

'I'm sure I can', he said, and so began her swimming career at eighty-six years of age!

At eighty-seven, Margo entered her first Master's Games, and when we met, she'd won 194 gold medals. Margo just looked at us with a slightly wicked twinkle in her eye, wiggled her finger and said, 'Don't tell me you're too old to try something new.'

So, I no longer had an excuse *not* to write my book. Thanks to Margo's inspiration, I began interviewing people aged eighteen to seventy-nine years old, who spend their lives in wheelchairs and finally **What we're Wheelie like**[10] went from dream to reality.

---

10   http://gailruthmiller.com/

I learnt so much during the interviews, and I thought I already knew a lot because of Mum's history, but that only scratched the surface. I learned of the everyday issues – like going to use a wheelchair-accessible toilet, only to find that it was being used as a storeroom. Or not being able to go on the bus with other students on a school excursion, because there is no ramp onto the bus, so you either stay at school, or go with your Mum. Boring! Or people having to wake up at 6.30 because that's when the carer arrives to do their showering. For a school child, this means no sleep-ins and no sleep-overs unless they're at their own house and that's not so much fun. If you can't get out of bed without a carer's help, then you can't raid the fridge for a midnight feast either!

Guess the one common attribute of all the interviewees?

They are all happy, well-adjusted, intelligent and fun-loving people, with a great attitude to life and the ability to find the positives in their situation. The difference is that they use a wheelchair instead of legs to get around.

This doesn't mean it's all roses, or that it's been an easy ride. One lady said, 'You won't believe what a girl said to her mum when we went on the school tour at the beginning of high school. She pointed to me and said, "Hey Mum isn't this cute? They even have kids in wheelchairs!" Can you believe she said that? I felt like a circus act!'

The interesting thing was that no-one I interviewed really moaned about their hassles. Yes, they were sometimes frustrated by some issues and the thoughtlessness of some people, but basically, they love to be independent, not molly-coddled and they just get on with life.

They don't like to be called amazing or inspirational, because they see themselves, just like the rest of us, but sitting down.

A female friend in her twenties who uses a wheelchair, has the most amazing collection of shoes, just like my daughter, Heidi, who's two years younger. As far as I can see the only difference between the girls is that one walks and the other wheels!

FOURTEEN

Intermissioned. Take 1

by Neville Hiatt.

Perspective is a powerful thing.

The first draft of my story for this project opened with:

8th July 2008 5:45 p.m. and my leather-encased body is sliding down the highway crossing lanes as I slide over the bitumen wondering when a car will run over the top of me.

That was the opening line of the last time my story was published in an anthology and so much has changed since then. I'd like to say my medical prognosis had too, but alas this is not the case. Any medical opinion I can access still says: 'medically retired for life'.

In 2008, my life changed in a second. I didn't expect my life would change again exactly 3,770 days later when I attended a healing meeting at my local church. I went to the meeting with zero expectations and nothing to lose. I was used to pain that was only relieved by lying on the floor in the back of the room during service. And now through a miracle from God, I am able to sit again without feeling like someone had spilled a box of thumbtacks on my seat before I sat down.

Before I get too much more into what my life is like now allow me take you back to the beginning. All the way back to when Ev birthed Kev. Kev then met Bev, and together they birthed me, Nev.

Kev and Bev should never have started a relationship let alone a family. They were both trying to escape their own childhoods by doing so. They did the best they knew how but essentially, Nev had to make himself. Drawing from hundreds of authors across thousands of pages, he used their words until he could form his own. All through primary school and high school these imaginary worlds were where Nev lived. It was safer there.

It's only in the last couple of years that I've come to appreciate just how much my childhood has impacted how I dealt with being medically retired by age thirty.

Growing up, I lived in the worlds of other authors, as an escape and a coping mechanism—reading stories of detectives and the Wild West, where there was always somebody willing to do the right thing even if they had some very evident shortcomings. There was always a solution at the end, and the right people always triumphed.

As a child, I thought it was just the stories I liked. Looking back, it's no surprise I was attracted to these stories when my own world was out of control with no solutions to be found.

The struggle I faced after the accident was the difficulty focusing and concentrating. It was hard to read and stay in a story. Movies were a workaround, but there is nothing quite like visualising a world for yourself for the first time.

Those same difficulties were ones I face in writing my own stories, including this one. With a half-asleep brain and a stiff, tight and exhausted body, needing to constantly change positions and breathe through the pain, getting words on the screen was a constant battle. Those difficulties are one of the reasons I applied to be a part of this project. If no one who faced challenges in life shared their story, how would we find encouragement and inspiration to persevere through whatever we are faced with?

I can still remember seeing *Avatar* after the accident and that moment when Jake Sully runs in his avatar body for the first time. To be pain-free and able to run again, a happy thought. Thankfully I'm not as blue as I was back then. Getting through a movie at the cinema was rarely worth the pain.

One of the biggest difficulties I faced in processing my emotions after the accident was that another of my previous coping mechanisms was no longer available to me. Growing up, exercise was a key escape. We all know that exercise is good for your mental health, not just physical wellbeing. I used exercise more than I ever realised to work through things, which I found out recently while working with a counsellor. The conundrum was that exercise made the pain worse, which was counter-productive to keeping my thought-life in a healthy place. I had to learn a lot about pacing. I missed and grieved for the ability to make my body feel something different through the strain of pushing it to its limits. Still, I was thankful that having been a state-level athlete in my formative years gave me an advantage in having a healthier body later in life.

Being able to walk now without needing to use the shopping cart as a support is so liberating. Sitting through an entire church service rather than lying down the back during the sermon still feels surreal. After ten years I'd grown so accustomed to what was my new normal that months after being healed my new new-normal is messing with my head. I can now do things I used to be able to do pre-accident. My body however has been very quick to remind me that after ten years of little activity, I need to walk before I jog, and jog before I run. Our bodies are so adaptive but not every adaptation is a healthy one.

One of the greatest assistants over the years was finding out about 'Grow'. Having its roots in the Alcoholics Anonymous' twelve-step program, it's been honed over the years to provide a well-rounded structure to assist in learning things about mental health and emotions that would have been great to learn at school. From perspective to pacing, to helping others at the same time, the months when I attended those weekly meetings definitely helped me keep going when my isolation was at its worst and finances at their lowest. As a free weekly meeting, despite no professionals being present, I found the group to be extremely beneficial in keeping a healthy perspective on life. The community and meeting regularity really helped me in moving forward rather than slipping past the point of no return.

The moment that really catapulted me to where I am today happened a couple of years ago when someone (almost in passing) told me about a guy named Dan Mohler. They were listening to his recordings to help them through what they were going through. One thing I had plenty of since the accident was time. I decided to use some of this time while lying on my bed to listen to some of Dan's YouTube videos. Over the weeks and months that followed I sensed I had changed and was continuing to change. Even now I find it hard to explain to someone else, but it was like what he said sank past the levels the shrinks and counsellors had been able to touch and changed lifelong things without me having to do any work. Even some of my closest friends noticed an overall change in me. To this day I continue to listen to HCSKL, which is a school that Dan Mohler ran in the USA a few years ago. Just this week I started listening again from day one with a friend and the content still resonates with me so strongly.

One of the biggest changes is finally being able to say, after thirty-eight years, I am single. By this I don't mean alone, I mean a *single*. A whole, unique individual not requiring someone else to fill gaps in my life. Every life choice up to this point had been made from a broken heart. A shattered spirit that was searching for comfort any way it could get it. It's wonderful now to feel this complete. To know what peace feels like and to no longer live based on my feelings is liberating, knowing that now I am finally ready for a relationship, yet ironically now I have no need of one, has me smiling.

So often over the years after the accident, I had the recurring thought of *I am glad I don't have kids or a wife as I'm struggling to take care of me, I would have nothing to give them in every sense of the phrase*. Then there were times I longed so badly for someone just to be there, to lighten the burden during the harder days. Having grown up a very independent and self-reliant person can have its benefits and drawbacks. Now, I look forward to what the future may hold, and yet feel so content now it really doesn't matter what happens in this regard. I am alone but no longer lonely.

Being able to take care of myself without needing to frequently go back to bed to recover, I'm even more hopeful for a future relationship There was nothing stopping me from having one while surviving but it sure narrowed the field of prospective wives. Now I can visit friends without needing to leave before the pain levels make it unsafe for the return journey, so I can socialise a lot more.

Another difficult challenge to deal with was losing the voice that I'd had when my radio career was intermissioned due to the accident.. It was a suggestion from my psychologist that despite my daily difficulties I needed to find a new voice for my creative talents and abilities. This started my journey from a hobbyist author and photographer to internationally-translated author and award-winning photographer. None of these endeavours aided in the financial burden of not being able to work, but they did help keep me alive. I still desperately would love the ability to work in a traditional sense again. Culturally, as an Aussie man, having that ripped away from me was one of many difficult adjustments I had to make.

Part of the journey to becoming a recognised artist was linking in with the local community radio station who are not only big supporters of the arts in the area, but also have a weekly radio show hosted by guys with various disabilities. The thing is, despite the numerous times they have interviewed me, if you were to ask me what their disabilities are, I could not accurately tell you. I could hazard a guess for some of them, but that's not the point. I have only ever known them for their abilities.

In spite of the hand they were dealt in life, they are doing something many would say they couldn't do. They have inspired me to keep going, and they have told me I have inspired them, so it's been a very symbiotic relationship. A relationship that was both beautiful and confronting at the same time. Every time I was asked to be on the show, I was reminded I used to once sit on the other side of the desk: switched on, happy and alert for hours on end. On the other side of the desk now, even a few minutes of clear thought to convey what I wanted to say was a challenge. The words would try and fight their way out of the fog and project out of my mouth without getting jumbled in between. I recently reposted some old behind-the-scenes videos from one of my photo series, and it's not easy accepting that reflection of myself. I guess that's what led me to shoot my first award-winning image, even if it took a year to achieve that title which is a story of perseverance in itself.

With the brief of producing an artwork of a local by a local for an exhibition that ran alongside the Archibald Prize when it toured Ballarat, I decided to tell my own story and shot the below image entitled "me 09_08_2015".

Twelve months after that exhibition, with the photo living in the garage in its box (too confronting for me to look at), I submitted it for another exhibition and this time it won first place. Now it hangs in someone's private collection.

Even typing, I would get words out of place or miss words, which was one of the reasons I kept my work to short stories and poems to combat these difficulties. Often I was left putting my breathing exercises into practice, because calling it frustration would be minimising the anger I felt at not being able to operate at the level I knew I was previously capable of.

Even now I get frustrated not being able to do what I want to be able to do.

Years of dedication and hard work and perseverance have seen multiple book titles—both solo and multi-author books bearing my name. I've had a string of exhibitions that could make a gallery owner think I was able to run a marathon (it's still on my bucket list despite the medical opinion). Maybe next year a marathon might actually happen; a lot of reconditioning has to happen first. My body is still getting used to sitting again.

Looking back on the last few years of being a photographer and author, part of me still wonders how I managed to be in thirty one exhibitions and have my short story collection translated into four languages. And then I marvel at how photography introduced me to an adventure in blockchain.

I was asking a gallery owner about exhibiting in their gallery a couple of years ago, and our conversation morphed into talking about 'trading forex', and then they mentioned Bitcoin. Having never heard of it before but always on the lookout for an opportunity to be able to provide for myself, I went home and spent hundreds of hours, again lying in bed, but this time learning about blockchain and cryptocurrencies. Just like in the art world where one exhibition can lead to another, and one contact can lead to a new publishing deal, I quickly started learning from some of the most knowledgeable people in the industry. The open and free sharing in this community has gone a long way to restoring my faith in people when it has been so battered after dealing with lawyers, corrupt insurance companies and people taking advantage of my diminished capacities for so many years.

So when I wrote the first draft of this story last year, the pain hadn't changed. Being away from home or trying to deal with any stress were still triggers for anxiety. Being on the motorbike was still a challenge when the conditions started to replicate those of the accident, and even on warm sunny days, short distances were all I could travel. But being able to share with others what I have learned was a refreshing change to the previous ten years—even if they had to come to my house because sometimes I couldn't get to them.

Having struggled to keep a roof over my head with my ability to earn a living taken away from me, it's been empowering to see a more promising future as well as being able to share that knowledge with others. This has given me a renewed sense of purpose. I now look forward to being able to afford better healthcare (without having to fight the insurance companies for months to obtain it) and taking care of myself the way I deserve. It's amazing the difference it has made in every facet of my life to see myself for who I was created to be, rather than who society has brainwashed me into believing I am. Beyond my own immediate world I am also excited about the impact blockchain can have on those who can most benefit from it. To be a part of the revolution that will see millions of unbanked people being able to transact in ways previously unavailable to them is exciting. Witnessing entire communities' wellbeing improve as their properties are titled and put on the blockchain giving them verifiable ownership for the first time. Beyond the price headlines are the stories that should be the lead story but aren't sensational enough.

Since starting to write this story, I've been reminded in a very real way just how valuable sharing our experiences can be. Someone I used to be very close to before my accident, and for a few months afterwards, recently reached out to me as they were dealing with a painful illness. Their thought process was: 'I remember Nev dealing with pain and maybe he can help me get through this stage of my life'. It's moments like this that make me thankful for what I've been able to gain from some of the experiences I've had in my life. There is no doubt that my life would have been easier if I wasn't bullied and abused as a child, raped as an adult, knocked off my bike ten years ago with the subsequent trauma and ordeals

I've faced since, including a breakdown at work. But as I discussed recently with my psychologist, there is a difference between knowledge gained from a textbook and something we have lived.

I will forever be thankful that my life didn't end that night; it was only intermissioned.

That was how my story ended when I first submitted it. Now my life is moving beyond the intermission: it's time for a new chapter.

I already had a fairly high level of appreciation for life before surviving the accident. This appreciation was heightened by not only surviving a situation that could have ended a lot differently, but also because of the journey I've been on since then. I tell people that I am thankful for the healing that took place in church that day; but as important as it was, it was only the icing on the cake. That 'cake' had been baking for the previous two years and that is where the greater healing has taken place.

Sleeping better and without the fatigue of being in so much pain all day has me looking forward like never before. Will I spend the final chapters of my life with someone to share my journey with? Will I be able to re-enter the workforce? Can I write a full-length novel or screen play? This may sound weird, but in some ways, at least mentally being healed after so long is almost as difficult to deal with as being so incapacitated.

After learning how to live life a certain way for what was a quarter of my life, I now appreciate what I had before the accident in a way I never could at the time. Now I know the value of life and won't be wasting a single second of the rest of my life. The accident still changed my life forever, but along the way I found my true identity.

FIFTEEN

Balancing Act
by Kathryn Hall and Rachel Mann

KATHRYN'S LIFE BECAME MORE INTERESTING NINE YEARS AGO when she joined a theatre company on a whim. Her path took a turn when she saw a show at the No Strings Attached Theatre of Disability based at Stepney, a suburb just outside of the city of Adelaide, South Australia. Within three months she had joined the company and within a further three months had been offered her own video project. More projects followed and before long Kathryn found herself tutoring others on a regular basis, travelling interstate and to regional South Australia to perform in original plays and to run acting workshops. She also began providing administrative support which led to her taking up a permanent administration volunteer role over the next seven years. Additionally, Kathryn has been involved in several Community Service Expos for the

National Disability Insurance Scheme (NDIS) to showcase the work of No Strings Attached in the disability sector.

Kathryn credits her venture into tutoring to the company's former Artistic Director, PJ Rose, who gave her 'the tutoring gig'. PJ Rose saw Kathryn's potential in the industry and encouraged her to complete a Certificate III in Arts Administration and a Certificate III in Event Management. Kathryn appreciated the support of someone who believed in her, and she has since flourished on her new path.

Kathryn now sees herself as an actor, and she loves it. And Kathryn is a young woman with cerebral palsy. She has some challenges which many take for granted, particularly her sense of balance, which in her words, 'Is not good; I fall over and break things and sprain things.' Fortunately, she has a high tolerance for pain! She also has a less than perfect memory for a woman of her age, and her stamina is sorely challenged at times from the effort required just to get around when her body is not in perfect harmony or sync with her mind and will.

Kathryn's journey into acting has not been straightforward, and certainly not an obvious choice. Kathryn was the second eldest of four children, with an older sister and a younger brother and sister. She describes her early years as being filled with endless appointments, going to all kinds of therapy, and overseen by a devoted mother who often worked three jobs to fund all the therapy appointments. The jobs often included night shifts so her mother would be available to take Kathryn to her appointments during the day. Kathryn's dad worked as a painter and 'built things' in her growing-up years. She was an independent young woman, moving out of home at sixteen years old, and opting to stay in South Australia when her family moved interstate. She initially found accommodation in a youth shelter but then received assistance to move into her own government-subsidised unit, which she still has today.

Leaving home at a young age to forge her own path provides a glimpse of Kathryn's early resilience and desire to steer away from any predictable route, and particularly so for a young woman with a disability. Kathryn described this time as one where she had to learn 'real quick' about her disability. She explained, 'Up to then everyone took care of me. I had to start taking care of myself'. Kathryn found a book about cerebral palsy in her school library and read everything she could about it, taking the book to her Occupational Therapist appointment so she could discuss it and understand it more.

Her memories of high school were that 'it sucked!' On a physical level, her hands cramped when she wrote which affected her writing and neatness, and for this, she was always penalised by her teachers. On a social level, there were no friends who welcomed and accepted her or who were interested in getting to know her and school consequently was a place of extreme loneliness and isolation. Kathryn's short-term memory problems and cerebral palsy were enough for some people to think of her as 'a big joke' and that she was lacking in intelligence. Kathryn remembers that she never found her 'niche'.

Her schooling years were unsurprisingly lacking in positive memory or experience. That is until she discovered dance and swimming in Year Twelve. These two interests gave her a feeling of being able to do something where she wasn't judged by anything else, only by what she was doing. She had a boost of confidence and a sense of accomplishment and decided she wanted to be a dancer. It was just what she needed to remind herself that she was perfectly capable of taking on new challenges and even unexpected pursuits for a young woman with cerebral palsy. It was the beginnings of seeing herself differently and of shaping a new path for herself.

For as long as she could remember, Kathryn had been driven to work hard. Looking back on her life, Kathryn described herself as an 'all or nothing' girl, throwing herself into new interests and dancing or gym, only to wear herself out after overdoing things in her first attempt. Her cerebral palsy had given her the drive to push herself beyond her limits to prove she could do as much as those without it, and she had held the view *as long as I work hard, I can achieve anything*. But with this determination and pressure to achieve came exhaustion. Kathryn found herself forced to confront the mindset she held which told her she could take on anything and that working hard was enough. She instead had to modify it to incorporate an acceptance of her limitations and to be mindful of her energy levels. In short, she had to pace herself. With this new mindset, she was learning to be more realistic about her capabilities and much kinder to herself in the process. After this period of reflection, she developed a new mantra of *you can do it tomorrow*, which she still reminds herself of when she is tempted to run ten kilometres on the treadmill at the gym!

It was during this time of personal discovery about her disability that Kathryn acknowledged that she did not have the build or balance to be a dancer. She had enjoyed dancing, but she was happy to let it go. With a more balanced approach to life came a desire to be more selective about how she spent her time and her energy. She pondered what she could enjoy doing and what she could be good at. It had to be something worth the effort she put into it and be something that she could enjoy and pursue into the future. When Kathryn saw a play at No Strings Attached in 2009, the stage was set to welcome in something new.

Before long, Kathryn found herself attending workshops at No Strings Attached and volunteering in the office. By the time she formally joined the theatre company three months later, she had already found it to be the long-awaited place of acceptance and belonging she had unknowingly been seeking; it also provided a sense of purpose and meaning to her days where she could shine, help others, and get on with something that she loved. Her ideas and experiences were valued and sought after, both to inform performance pieces and to train others in their own acting journey. She was good at acting. She had found her niche. She couldn't have asked for more.

There were some hurdles, but she once again rose to the challenge. If she wanted to be a talented actor, she had to work on her speech and ensure it was clear. She learned that she was 'in her head' a lot and that to be a good actor, she had to reverse this and operate more from her heart. She was willing to do what she had to do as she sensed that this was going to be something long lasting and worthy of her full commitment. Before No Strings Attached, it had been hard for her to find to find the right fit of something to focus on and stick with. She tried a new interest for a few months or a year, but then it wouldn't go anywhere. One of these pursuits included writing, but she found it too solitary. She liked the support she received at No Strings Attached and the opportunity to bounce ideas off others. She also liked participating in the creative process. And collaborating. This 'gig' wasn't like the other things she had tried. Acting felt different. It felt like it was here to stay.

Kathryn's life has been full and busy since those early days of joining No Strings Attached. She has performed in mixed doubles workshops, performing and touring to the Awakenings Festival in Horsham, Victoria, and was invited to join the No Strings Attached professional training program called Preparing the Garden where she participated in several creative developments and completed a short film on disability and dating. She is also a founding member of the No Strings Attached Women's Ensemble which performed at the 2016 Adelaide Fringe Festival.[11]

Kathryn has recently been co-writing and performing in a production about memory and the difficulties some people face in their day to day lives when they have memory problems. Alirio Zavarce, the Artistic Director of No Strings Attached, described how he found inspiration for the play after an experience Kathryn shared with him of being on a bus and forgetting whether she was travelling to the city or travelling home from the city. Together they began looking at the process of memory—how details can be forgotten, and how they are remembered. They particularly wanted to explore 'those areas of life which contribute to the forgetting or the remembering' whether it be through birth, medication, accident or illness. Their discussions progressed and evolved further with more collaborators Michaela Cantwell, Cassie Litchfield, Duncan Luke and Kym Mackenzie into the piece called *I Forgot to Remember to Forget*.

The play was performed at the True Colours Festival in Singapore, March 2018. Alirio described Kathryn as 'a brilliant and amazing performer and collaborator' and the play as 'simply beautiful'. Kathryn described how she and the three other performers in the play wanted to make sure it was 'something really special'. Being on stage with lights, sound cubes and 'tech guys', as well as the visual projections which added further to the impact of the performances, gave Kathryn an 'added buzz'. Director Alirio described the play as: 'An innovative, fun and touching exploration about the lived experience of memory loss'

---

11   No Strings Attached website, viewed 2016.

explaining how the play 'explores resilience, how we deal with and accept change, how sometimes we have to re-learn everything and how sometimes we forget it all. He elaborates further that, 'It is a reminder of our responsibility as friends, family and a society to remember the value and place of the individual in community, even when they themselves might not remember any more.'

Australian-based theatre director Shona Benson described the play as 'A work that has been gently and delicately brought to life and the result is a deeply touching and enchanting piece of theatre'.

When describing the feeling of being on stage Kathryn says, 'It's amazing. I still get the after-performance buzz and I am usually bouncing off the walls.' The day after a big performance finds Kathryn sleeping all day to recover from the intensity of the experience, but she says she loves 'the intense concentration for short bursts of time and the feel of being in that headspace; the experience of working so hard to fine tune it and to see it all come together is both an interesting and lovely experience'. Kathryn and the cast are performing the play at the at the Adelaide Festival Centre for its Australian Premiere in July 2019.

Kathryn auditioned for and won a small role in the film *Rabbit* which was released in August 2017 at the Melbourne Film Festival and was showcased at the Fantastic Fest in Texas. The Fantastic Fest describes itself as a festival dedicated to championing challenging and thought-provoking cinema, celebrating new voices and new stories from around the world as well as supporting new filmmakers. The Director, Luke Shanahan, set the movie in South Australia, with the story of twins, one who goes missing, possibly kidnapped and of the estranged twin's exploration for her missing sister. It is described as a haunting thriller which explores the connections between twins through a 'science fiction lens, tinged with elements of horror.'[12]

Indeed, Kathryn's character was intended to be found dead in a forest, and in preparation she endured several hours of having special-effects make up applied to make her look like she was decomposing. To add to the sense of foreboding and all things ominous, there was a fierce storm on the night her part was due to be filmed, ending filming prematurely and making the forest hazardous with copious amounts of mud. Kathryn spent hours waiting for the storm to pass in freezing conditions before they called it quits on her scene due to the unfavourable weather. Kathryn remembers the storm was so severe that it caused a state wide power blackout for twelve hours the following day.

On a previous day, Kathryn had filmed a scene in the forest, wearing high heels, which meant each step had to be carefully navigated to avoid sinking down into the sludgy mud. Kathryn's cerebral palsy had presented her with a lifelong challenge to keep her balance and so she was incredulous that she had been able to keep her balance during this scene.

Although not all Kathryn's scenes made it into the movie, the experience was overall eye-opening in terms of the realities and less-glamorous side of movie making. It was also an experience of personal discovery. It brought to her attention her impressive resilience, perseverance and stamina under pressure and gave her an experience of overcoming the challenges of her disability, against all the odds.

Kathryn is inspired by the notion that *you never know what you can do until you try to do it*, stating, 'I'm all for people dreaming, but you have to take that step up and attempt to do it, even when you crash and burn in a spectacular way'. Something that inspires

---

[12] Fantastic Fest website 2017

her the most in people is their mission to work hard, especially when it is despite their limitations, as she strives to do. Kathryn explains, 'I like it when people give things a try, and to not just try but to keep on trying to try!' With her own life, she is aware of the importance of having goals and keeping focused on them in order to achieve anything that is important to herself.

When talking about the greatest impacts of her disability, Kathryn explains that a lot of the 'managing' of her disability is to do with energy conservation and realising that she cannot 'do everything every day'. Her second challenge is how she manages that with others, explaining that, 'for the longest time I've been meek and mild but now I'm gaining confidence to say what I need and wanting people to take what I say seriously'. She has been working on that fine line between assertiveness and aggression, trying to get her needs met without upsetting others in the process. When considering her future in acting, Kathryn hopes there will be more professional paid acting roles for her and that she will have the courage to go to more open auditions.

When pondering how she wishes to live her life, Kathryn explains that she is 'still working on it'. She admits to being stubborn, but this has worked to her advantage and spurred her on to never give up on herself. She looks to Steven Bradbury, the Australian speed skating Gold Medal Olympian, as an inspiration, explaining that, 'just because he had a bit of luck on his side, it doesn't mean he didn't work hard to get there'. Kathryn feels a deep affinity for his story and loves how he did his best and embraced the positive. It's a story that provides inspiration in other ways too—that you never know what may happen despite all the obstacles, setbacks and extra challenges in your path.

Kathryn has proven this over and over through the years. She has challenged herself despite the limitations of her disability.

Her disability is factored into her life in a way that respects the limitations it presents, and keeps Kathryn open to how it can also create new, different and exciting opportunities. Without it, her life may be on a different path. She has not only made the best of it but also discovered how it can be put to use. Kathryn's hard work and independent spirit have unleashed the unexpected and forged a path that will no doubt inspire others to think outside the square when it comes to living with a disability.

Kathryn's plans for her future, however, are simple, realistic and wise, and come from someone who has learned over time that it pays to stick with what works best. And for Kathryn, what works for her and keeps everything running smoothly is keeping her life in balance. Kathryn now considers her primary focus as being 'to take care of myself'. She is looking forward to NDIS services helping make life easier so she can look after herself better. She hopes to be employed and earning money, doing something that she enjoys and is looking forward to what comes next. At this stage, she isn't 100% sure what that is but is open to new opportunities that come along. In the meantime, her desire is to 'keep working hard, to rest when needed' and to stick to her motto 'to always try'.

SIXTEEN

Behind Closed Doors

by Melinda Jones and David Wayne Wilson

WHETHER WALKING THROUGH THE STREETS, SHOPPING centres, or sitting on a park bench, we all observe strangers. We are people-watchers. We examine people's posture, gait, behaviour and speech. Why do we do this? Are we intrigued by what we see? And do we judge before knowing the truth about the person?

I try to avoid making judgements about people, including making comments about them. Instead, I try to get to know the person, and offer help, support or assistance. I wish people could have done this for me, rather than judging me for many years. No one knows what goes on behind closed doors, such as the door to my home. Everyone is unique and has their own story to tell. Some stories are filled with happiness, joy, love, laughter, and hardships, the usual life ups and downs. Another person's life could be one of complete sadness. Perhaps they suffer from depression, anxiety, medical issues, mental illness, homelessness, abuse or have a disability.

My name is Melinda, and my story is lived and written behind closed doors. I am opening my door to share my life with you.

I am forty years old and am permanently deaf. I wear a cochlear implant on my left ear to assist with my hearing. Some people have benefited from using an implant, however, my situation is different. The cochlear implant does not give me the quality of hearing that users would expect, as the sound I hear is robotic with white noise. It takes an immense amount of concentration to understand what people are saying, and I experience nerve fatigue from wearing it. The implant was inserted during recent brain surgery, and it has not been as successful as the specialist and I had hoped. Our family uses sign language for communication on a daily basis.

I have brain tumours as a result of Neurofibromatosis Type 2 (NF2). I was born with this genetic disorder, and growths can grow anywhere within my nervous system. Our bodies are made up of a complex system of nerves, and knowing I could have tumours growing at any location regularly overwhelms my thinking.

Brain surgery is invasive, and successive operations have affected my vestibular system, so I have difficulty keeping my balance when I walk. I have a condition called 'Oscillopsia', leading to vision impairment as I walk where everything I see jumps up and down, and I am unable to focus. This makes walking pretty much a guessing game. When I stop walking, my eyes regain focus, and I can see again That's a great feeling! I am forever guessing at who is approaching me, and I need to stop to respond back. I feel so silly at times.

I feel as if I am jumping on a pogo stick or having a wild ride on a rollercoaster, and the constant movement of my body, especially my head, causes me great distress. This is the norm for me, part of my everyday life; it is ongoing, and it is mine forever. Often I want to raise my hands and yell to the world, 'Please make it stop!'

I feel that I am fortunate that I have only required two brain surgeries to remove tumours. However, they have caused permanent deafness and spinal pain. There are six additional tumours: some are stable while others are monitored closely. A few are inoperable due to their proximity to other organs, and I am playing the waiting game and thinking about what to do next. NF2 tumours can grow incredibly fast without warning. I may develop others in my body at any given time.

I had had enough. Enough of *what* you may be asking? It was the judgements, bullying, criticism and the feeling of being ignored. I'd also had enough of feeling weak, fatigued, worn out, nauseated, sick and unwell; of the vertigo attacks and the subsequent falling and bumping into anything and everything. I regularly had bruises and the ringing of tinnitus in my ears. I'd had enough of the constant stomach issues brought on by the medication used to combat my pain with a drug that feels as if it is chewing up my stomach lining; and it probably is. I'd had enough of numbness in my face as well as facial twitching. My taste buds have been damaged and have never returned to their normal state, so food does not taste the same as I remember. I loved my food! I'd had enough of feeling sad, lonely and not fitting in with the society I once knew, as I was left out of social outings and gatherings. When I became deaf, I was cut off from the rest of the world.

People almost stopped checking in to see how I was doing. There were no more girls' nights out, music concerts nor parties once I became completely deaf. NOTHING! A few people stopped communicating via text messages and email, as they preferred phone calls, but they knew that making phone calls was almost impossible for me. Perhaps my sense of isolation was due to people not understanding how to communicate with me. It was hurting me and cut me deeply, further affecting my mental health.

I felt invisible and began to lose all sense of identity. I was still grieving for the loss of my hearing that I'd had for thirty-eight years. A part of me died that day on the operating table. It was a similar experience as losing a mother, father or a loved one. How long does it take to grieve? My self-esteem continued on a downward spiral. *Who was I now? Why me? Why now?* No one was listening, and I had no answers to my questions. Although I had a beautiful family with three young children aged ten, nine and seven years, I began to feel numb, and my existence was disappearing from the world as I could no longer hear my children's voices.

I was continually looked down upon, stared at and frowned at because I had a disability. I didn't want to know about the reality of what my life was. Following the operation that left me deaf, I received a visitor who waved hello and began to talk to me. My husband explained my situation.

'I'm sorry, but Mel is deaf now, she cannot hear you, please use the whiteboard and pen to communicate with her. She can write back to you'.

The visitor waved their arms in the air refusing to use the whiteboard, and they pushed the whiteboard away replying, 'No way! I'm not doing that'.

The look of disgust on that visitor's face made my heart sink. Lip-reading is a difficult skill to acquire and people in my life were getting frustrated with me as I was continually asking them to repeat themselves. The whiteboard was now my means of communicating with everyone, and it was such an excellent tool to use to communicate with the medical staff. I didn't ask to be deaf, nor want to be deaf, and I felt sick at the number of people that gave up on me.

Due to my disabilities, I received a disability parking permit, and people gave me stares, frowns and hurtful comments when I used the specially-marked bays. My health issues were invisible, and many people expected to see a wheelchair or at least a limp to validate the use of the carpark.

'You are fine; you don't look disabled to me, so get out of that bay and give it to someone who deserves it'.

The old saying comes to my mind: 'Never judge a book by its cover'.

I didn't want to offend, and each time I apologised, my eyes would fill up with tears. I tried to stay strong, and hold back the tears while my thoughts were tormenting me, destroying my soul from within. And then there was the pain and the medication I had to take every day. With my body failing me, and people treating me differently, I hated myself; the little self-esteem that I had left, vanished. Tears rolled down my left cheek: past brain surgery destroyed the tear duct in my right eye. All of the hurt had pushed me to the edge of survival. What did I do to deserve this? What did I do to deserve to be treated differently or to be judged? I can be strong because I need to be, to hold up appearances. But I was so tired …

I believed I was an inconvenience to others, being deaf and not being able to drink, or party and all that goes with going out in loud social environments. I withdrew from all social occasions as I wasn't coping. I felt helpless, lost weight and became too skinny; I had no energy, and my sleeping patterns were erratic. I realised that my disability was a burden not only to myself but to others as well.

When I talked to others about my feelings, they responded with, 'At least you are only deaf and not blind' or 'Deal with it, get over it, it's not the end of the world'. I could not explain nor express myself without getting put down, hurt, criticised and judged. People don't want to know when you are not coping; they only want to know when you are. When you look good from the outside, you must be healthy on the inside. I had to gather all my inner strength and resilience to fight off all that was being said and done. I believe in the power of the mind and believe in my ability to overcome all obstacles in my way to set myself free. Sometimes life challenges my self-belief.

There have been times I thought about ending my life. I remember one such time well. I was physically down due to my health issues, and my mental state had deteriorated due to the negativity directed at me. I walked out of my front door onto the road and onto the median strip. I live on a busy street and cars were driving past me quickly. As I watched the vehicles approach from a distance, I was calculating when to jump in front of them. *Do I jump out in front of this car or wait for the next?* I wanted to end my life, rather than cause damage. Do I choose a bigger car, or maybe a bus or a truck?

I would watch the traffic for hours, waiting for the best moment to end my life. The only reason that would stop me was my three beautiful children. Their eyes glistening at me, smiles of comfort, expressions of laughter, hand written notes of love and encouragement, and their hugs made me take a step back from the curb. My children filled my heart with their love.

My eldest son regularly wrote to me as he has a gentle and pure soul.

'Mum, you are my hero, my love, my life, my role model, and always remember Mum never to give in or give up!'

I could not fathom my life without my children in it, nor their life without me. How could I end my life when I had so much to live for? Their love for me is strong, positive and powerful, and sends off the happy endorphins in my body.

Why did I allow others in this world to bring me to this point? Are they living my life? Do they realise what goes on behind my closed door? I once read: 'There will be many chapters in your life. Don't get lost in the one you're in now'[13]. How could I step away from the most important and valuable people in my life? My children, my husband, my family and closest friends. They are the ones who have stood by me and have supported me all along my journey with NF2 and deafness. My children and husband learned sign language to communicate with me, a language so special to us now. My family and friends raised money to allow me to have life-saving brain surgery and hearing preservation surgery. There are still six more brain tumours to contend with, and maybe more. I have so much to endure. However, I now have the love and support of these dear people still holding my broken heart together.

I ceased going to the road to find opportunities to end my life. Instead, I sat on the front porch of my house for reflection. I decided to get into a positive mind set. I could not control what was happening to me. I could not control my medical condition or deafness. But I could control how I could respond to it.

The pain of regret outweighs the pain of risk. I received counselling through my NDIS psychologist who showed me that the way to defeat isolation was to reach out. Simply talking about anything and everything was a relief and helped my mental health. It was a great way to release all the negativity that was gradually killing me from the inside.

I joined Facebook groups for the 'deaf' and 'cochlear implant personal experiences' and 'Acoustic Neuroma Association'. I

---

13 http://www.ryanintheus.com/change-by-chapters/ by Ryan Hodgson. Accessed March 2019.

regularly attended Acoustic Neuroma support meetings, as well as those at the Western Australian Deaf Association to improve my sign language. I felt welcome and normal, despite living with so many disabilities and medical conditions. The support of these groups was phenomenal! I was amazed how much weight was lifted off my shoulders by speaking out and reaching for help.

To help with healing my body, mind and soul, I placed more emphasis on my children and family. I commenced a blog about my health journey and included my surgeries with photographs. It was therapeutic and gave insight to others. They were able to read how life changed over time.

I received personal messages asking me for more information about my disabilities. People were intrigued by my experiences. Some people were diagnosed with similar conditions and were reaching out for help, support, care, compassion and knowledge.

Perhaps our journeys with disabilities have to be as long as it requires to inspire and give hope to other people living with similar issues. To share the reassurance that you are never alone, and we are here to support and hold each other when we cannot do it alone.

Knowing I can help others has given my life more meaning. Connecting with other people with the same or similar conditions, disabilities and medical issues, enabled me to find new friends and have a sense of belonging with them. It also gave me an appreciation for others with disabilities and backgrounds that I didn't know existed.

You could live next to a person who is broken or struggling with their personal problems, demons or disabilities and you wouldn't know it. You should always be kind to everyone you meet. Spend quality time with them, instead of judging them. It will make a world of difference to them.

My husband, children and I aim to go on two to three big camping trips a year. We make memories while I am fit and still able. No one can predict the future, such as the condition of my health. I am in control of fun times with my family, which adds to the memories my family can recall in the future. I am determined to connect with the world again, overcome obstacles, and achieve many goals in life.

On one camping trip we travelled to Western Australia's Pilbara and Gascoyne regions. I never thought I'd be walking up and down gorges, cliffs, tunnels and gullies. With the help of my steady hiking boots, knee braces and professionally-made walking aid hiking sticks, the feeling was sensational! The feeling was magical! You could not wipe the smile off my face, and tears of happiness flowed down my cheek. Once again, I was ALIVE and felt the emotions of achieving goals, even if much of it was achieved by shuffling on my bum and using my hands and knees for crawling and to keep my balance.

With determination, a positive mindset and a little stubbornness, I succeeded. My self-esteem and confidence were rising. Something I had not experienced in a long time.

The mind is a powerfully positive tool. Never underestimate your ability to find solutions to problems in life. Being positive and not giving in during low points in your life will reveal your true potential. These times will show you what you can achieve, not what you cannot. I am not allowing my disabilities to define me. We are all special, valuable and share remarkable talents and qualities. We all have our own special purpose in life. Do not let disability define you. Instead, you define it.

I would like to share a Facebook post which has a powerful message.[14] It changed my mindset, and now I live by it.

---

14 'Joy of Mum' https://www.facebook.com/joyofmom. Accessed March 2019.

Don't let this world make you bitter. Don't let the actions of other people turn you cold on the inside. Certain things happen to hurt us, people come and leave us, and most of all there are moments when you're bound to fall. Don't let those things make you unkind. It's ok to cry. It's ok to be sad. But it's never ok to do other people wrong just because you were done wrong. We're human. We break. We make mistakes. But don't let pain and sadness run your lives. Wake up in the morning and do what you think is right. There are moments in your life where you feel like giving up, and you can't take it anymore. It's ok. Breathe. Inhale. Exhale. I know you're weak. But the things that show your weak side are also the same ones that make you stronger in the long run. It's all about taking whatever life throws at you and learning from it.

Never let anyone take away the beauty that shines from your beautiful soul. The best kind of people are the ones who come into your life and make you see the sun and rainbows, rather than the dark grey clouds. The people who believe in you help you believe in yourself. They are the people that provide love, care and support and accept you the way you are. We all walk unique journeys in life. You may be reading this chapter and going through challenges in life. You may be tired and close to breaking. There is a strength within you. Keep fighting! You are beautiful, amazing and inspirational. Never lose hope. Maybe your door is closed and needs to be opened to share your life with someone else?

SEVENTEEN

Deaf, Blind and On the Catwalk
by Vanessa Vlajkovic

PUTTING MY LIFE DOWN ON PAPER SHOULD NEVER HAVE BEEN this hard to do. In fact, I thought it would be pretty easy to jot down all the highs and lows and hand it in. But when I finally mustered the courage to sit down and pour my soul out, I didn't have a clue where to begin. It's ironic because I'm only twenty-one years old as I write this—it's not as if I've survived two world wars or have that much to tell. Yet, I struggle to decide which events to include and which to leave out because I can't cover everything in this one chapter.

I have to confess that I've been through a lot, but when compared to other people's stories, mine seems somewhat trivial. I guess we are all special in our own way and each has something worth hearing. No doubt many of the stories in this book will make you cry, make you smile and laugh. And that's what I want—I want you to step into my shoes and walk in my footsteps for a few pages. I want you to feel my pain, my joy and every other emotion in between. So, get comfortable as I bring you behind the scenes of Ness Vlajkovic's life.

I was born with a condition called Optic Atrophy, which means that my optic nerve never formed correctly, and as a result, I am legally blind. I have twenty percent remaining vision, so I am not in total darkness. More like semi-blurriness but only when attempting to see things that aren't a couple of metres away. I am unable to read normal-sized writing, and at the age of four, I learnt Braille. This was to be my primary communication method for the next twelve years.

Vision loss aside, I was still the same as every little girl my age. I didn't visibly appear different so unless you knew me you wouldn't be aware of my disability. It was that subtle.

I did trial glasses at the age of five or six, but these were found to be ineffective, despite making me look super cute.

In kindergarten, I made friends like other children and even developed the bad habit of sucking my thumb after copying the girl who slept next to me. This later cost thousands of dollars in orthodontic bills, but in the end, I was just being an average child, copying my friend and knowing no better. It was much the same in pre-primary, however, this is the point at which things changed—I was tested by the school nurse and declared to be deaf. Well, they called it "hearing impaired" because it was very mild and could be helped with hearing aids. But hearing aids I did not want. I was fiercely against them, claiming they made me stand out. It took me many years to accept that I NEEDED them, and that other people's opinions didn't matter. Additionally, technology did keep improving, as it always does, and my hearing aids were frequently updated—meaning that by the time I got to high school they were so small and blended with my skin so that I wasn't bothered at all because they were well-hidden behind my long hair.

Primary school was a lonely affair. High school was even worse. Being in a mainstream school with a dual sensory loss was hardly a walk in the park. There were bullies and it was so very isolating. I did my best to fit in. For example, I played volleyball in Years Eight and Nine for the school team and competed in inter-school matches. I eventually realised that I would have to grin and bear it because there wasn't an alternative. It sucked; I wanted friends to hang out with, and I wanted people to like me. But teenagers are weird humans that you can't talk sense into. I got invited nowhere and never went to parties. In short, I was a loser. Or so I thought.

In my first two years of high school, my hearing took a nose-dive. It was quite gradual, but by the end of Year Nine, I was told an interpreter would be the solution. I was keen on this as I had seriously missed out on much of what was said to me until then and I was ready to embrace a new and beautiful language—Auslan.

Sometime during Year Ten I did some in-depth testing and was re-diagnosed—I now had Auditory Neuropathy Spectrum Disorder, quite a mouthful. My auditory nerve had broken, leaving me with inconsistent hearing and no use for hearing aids any more. This further confirmed the need to continue with an interpreter, and since then I have never looked back.

Sure, it was difficult to pick up a new language in the midst of study. But having English, Bosnian, Braille and Indonesian under my belt already, my fifth language was far smoother than it could have been. My family are from Bosnia, with my parents and brother being born there, so I learnt that at the same time as English. I began studying Indonesian in primary school and continued on through high school, thus resulting in ten years of learning and making me almost fluent. I had no official training in Auslan, and I didn't do classes or anything like that. I just learnt from other deaf people and my interpreters. It didn't take me very long to remember, and within twelve months I was fluent. I was now classified as 'deafblind'—maybe I was deafblind from the age of seven, but no one told me the terminology back then, so oh well.

There was one major drawback to all this excitement—my family were unhappy. They had pushed and begged for me to do what they wanted, which was to get a cochlear implant. This wasn't right for me, and I was fully opposed to it, but my family didn't and possibly never will understand my reasoning. It was a huge transition they hadn't been prepared for. They weren't thrilled that I wanted to connect with the deaf and deafblind community and immerse myself in their rich culture. They tried time and time again to persuade me that a cochlear implant would cure my deafness and I would be able to hear everything. But the trouble is, I didn't, and still don't, want to be healed. I'm not ill. My disabilities are not a debilitating disease that will kill me. (I'm going to die from some boring, natural cause instead.) I am extremely content the way I am and become highly offended when people suggest I need 'fixing'.

In summary, my relationship with my family has suffered, and I feel we have lost a bond we had before. This doesn't mean I don't still love them—I do. It has just led me to seek support from elsewhere.

Once I left school, I raked in a great group of friends who I am forever grateful to have in my life. These people understand my perspective, they encourage me and never express any negativity at my desire for freedom. I am not naming the people in this book for privacy reasons, but you know who you are, so I hope you know how much I appreciate your friendship.

I want to talk a bit about my hobbies and significant moments in my life. These are things I am proud of, and I try not to be too proud too often so it should not be taken as bragging.

Firstly, I have a background in dancing and gymnastics, with my current sport being cheerleading. I did jazz, tap, ballet, hip-hop, Spanish and acrobatics for close to a decade. I then did gymnastics for two years which admittedly was more for my Year Twelve exams than for recreational purposes. On completion of the exam, I decided cheerleading was more suited to me than bleeding hands from bars as a gymnast. It was good for me to move around and see what sport matched my abilities.

Other activities I enjoy in my downtime are reading, listening to Harry Styles, travelling and riding ridiculous roller coasters. I'm also the Vice President of the Board of Deafblind Australia and a committee member of the Youth Disability Advocacy Network, two advocacy groups—one specific to Western Australia and one being a national body. I'm so fortunate to be able to make change happen with these passionate individuals, and I think the future looks bright for them both.

In 2014 I began winning awards in the community—some local, some national and some international. I had never dreamed of attracting lots of attention—it just happened. Amid the list of awards are two Onkyo World Braille Essay Contest wins, Western Australia's Young Person of the Year and Deaf Australia's Young Person of the Year. On top of those, I have been in three beauty pageants and been crowned Miss Deaf Australia, Miss Deaf International (MDI) first runner-up and Miss West Coast Toybox Ambassador. These were all won between 2014-2018.

I travelled to Paris and Denmark in 2017, the former for the MDI mentioned above and the latter for a conference I presented at. In 2018 I went to England on a deafblind youth exchange program and Spain to present at another conference. I have also been to Switzerland for a Deafblind International Youth Network (DBIYN) event. 2019 sees me back to Paris to participate in the DBIYN's yearly social event with a December trip to Indonesia for eight weeks to participate in the Australian Indonesian Youth Exchange Program.

These experiences have allowed me to grow as a person and to teach myself the extent I am willing to go to for certain situations. They have shaped me and assisted me to become more confident and assertive in my daily life. They have given me the motivation to get out of bed every morning, knowing that I can make a difference if I smash out some barriers and never give up.

On the 31st of December 2018, I took a big leap—I moved out of my parents' home and into my best friend's place. This decision had been a long time coming but I had put it off due to knowing the drama it would cause and not being willing to deal with that kind of stress. By drama I mean, my family not being in agreement with me leaving, as they didn't deem me 'ready' for that sort of experience. I, however, was long past the ready stage. I was busting to get out and into the world, to become as independent as possible. That couldn't happen when I lived in a place where my every move was monitored, and I was forced to abide by rules that did not suit me in the slightest. I had to make some sacrifices when I made the choice to move out, as I had to leave my dog behind. This was probably the most difficult part for me because Edi, my beloved chihuahua, has provided me with much comfort and relief since he came into my life in 2012. To make myself feel better about how terribly I miss him, I keep reminding myself that

I will very soon have a Guide Dog so that will hopefully fill the void in my heart and give me something positive to focus my energies on.

Since living with my best friends, my general quality of life has dramatically taken a turn for the better and I have felt myself breathe for the first time in years. To anybody who is reading this and may have been put in similar circumstances, please don't feel stuck because you're sure as hell not alone in this. If you are unhappy in any area of your life, it's paramount to seek help and get what you want/need - you deserve to feel worthy, respected and most of all, not be stripped of your dignity.

Not living with my parents has of course been an adjustment for me, in the sense that I now rely on myself a lot more and have expanded my knowledge base on a great many levels. It's not to say there haven't been challenges, but I have always overcome them with my network of supportive individuals and have achieved numerous milestones in the months immediately following my new housing arrangement. One of these milestones is that I can now catch the bus and train basically anywhere, by myself. This was unheard of when I lived at home and I am so proud of myself (despite saying at the beginning of this chapter that I don't get proud often!) because it's been a goal of mine for so long, so seeing it come true was very exciting.

Another activity I want to share is that I have ticked sky-diving off my bucket list. I am either brave, crazy or both—but I will never forget the exhilaration as I jumped fourteen thousand five hundred feet from the sky. The best way to describe it is: holy fxxk. That was actually what I uttered mid-freefall, as well as other colourful expletives!

So where does that leave me?

At this present time, I am in my third and final year of undergraduate study at Edith Cowan University in Perth, WA. I am majoring in journalism with a public relations minor. Upon graduation in May 2019, I intend to apply for post-graduate study but am not yet sure where or what subject. I am currently holding down two part-time jobs while seeking a fulltime position.

But I am also just going with the flow and being a wild spirit—I'm not locking in any definitive future. Anything can happen and I'd rather let the wind blow me where it wants than plan something that later fails to work out. But if someone insists on knowing where I would like to be in ten years, my answer would be 'married with four kids and be doing something that I love as a career, whatever that may be by that time.' I would like to have travelled some more and made some fantastic memories before I'm thirty-one! I don't know what else to say, however, I would like to be a successful woman that people will recognise for the work I do. I want to leave my mark on society so that in a hundred years I won't be forgotten.

EIGHTEEN

Save The Drama for The Llama

by Zia Westerman and Pamela Farley

My name is Zia, and I am a writer. I love music, watching movies, speaking Spanish, going out for coffee and looking in the shops. One of my dreams is to one day own an Alpaca. My nickname at home is Llama!

I was born, along with my twin sister Cyanne, in the South Australian city of Whyalla. As babies, we were adorable cuddly-bundles and did everything other babies did. We could sit up and roll around. We used to hold each other's hands as we slept.

But my mother observed something wrong with our development at around one year of age; something different that she picked up in the way we moved around. The local doctors didn't agree and suspected her of paranoia, but about one week before we turned two years of age, we were diagnosed with Muscular Dystrophy.

Mum was right.

Once famed for steel and ship production, Whyalla is the third most populous town in the state. It is a long drive, over three hundred and eighty kilometres, to get to Adelaide and its medical specialists and facilities. The town never reached its predicted peak, and when the steel industry went into decline in the early 80s, many people moved away. Our town wasn't a 'disability-friendly city'; if it had been, our lives would have been easier. We spent a good many days travelling back and forward to Adelaide. These days were lengthy and costly for my family.

I attended kindergarten and then Memorial Oval Primary School. I went to both Stuart High School and Edward John Eyre High School, but there were stumbling blocks at each progression, and my mum was advised to send us to the 'Special School'. She refused and fought for us to attend mainstream schools. She argued that 'our illness affected our muscles, not our minds'.

My mother has always been there for us, but she has had to fight every inch of the way, especially as we grew older and our needs changed. By the age of ten we were in wheelchairs, manual ones to begin with, but as our muscles grew weaker, they were replaced with electric ones. My mum fought for every bit of help we now receive; from the equipment to the carers and the million-and-one other things in between. We are lucky she is so strong and loves us so much.

Although Cyanne and I are twins, I would say we are opposites. Cyanne is right-handed, and I am left-handed. Cyanne loves to wear black clothes and is the artistic one in the family. When we were growing up Cyanne and I had separate rooms. We would go into our room and pick out clothes for the day, but more often than not we would come out wearing the same thing. We still select similar clothing to wear. Cyanne has been a big part of my life, and she endures the same struggle as me.

A couple of years ago, a friend of mine who works in the council asked me to write about my everyday life. I wrote the following details, and it was read out in the South Australian Parliament.

A simple day in the life of Cyanne and Zia

Cyanne and I share a distinct feature. We are both redheads. If you live in Whyalla, you may have seen us zooming around the shops or sitting at a cafe drinking coffee with our wonderful carers. The people who are close to us know we have a bright outlook on life and a great sense of humour. They also understand the type of disability we have. For those of you who don't know, we live with a condition called Limb-girdle Muscular Dystrophy type 2i. It is a rare genetic condition that affects the core muscles.

Living with Muscular Dystrophy isn't hard; what is hard is relying on other people to assist us with everything we need or want to do. Total reliance is both difficult and frustrating. Cyanne and I don't like telling people the ins and outs of our private life, but in the last couple of years we have begun to share our world.

How will things change for the better if no one knows our story?

We want people to know about our daily struggles. Some of the simple things in most people's lives can be very troubling for us.

Our daily life is a time schedule from the moment we open our eyes in the morning to the moment we close our eyes at night. It is not our choice to live this way, but it is our only choice if we want to get out of bed in the mornings. The powers in charge of the disability system seem to think that it is okay for people with disabilities to have the same time schedule every day for the rest of their lives. Our amazing mum has fought for the care we have today, even though it is still not enough

At seven am we have two carers who come in to get us out of bed, take us to the toilet, shower and dress us. This may sound like an easy job, but it isn't. We have had many carers turn away because it is too hard or too confronting for them, never mind what it does to *our* emotional state.

Our carers have a no-lift policy and must use lifters like the ones you see at the hospital or aged care homes. It took me years to finally accept the fact that I have to use these things for the rest of my life. I know what it is like to walk and not have to deal with lifters and carers —a normal life— so adjusting to a dependent way of life was extremely hard. I still struggle to accept on some days.

It takes nearly an hour each for Cyanne and I to get ready in the mornings. This can take longer if we need to wash our hair and may vary with different carers. At ten a.m. we go to the toilet. We go two more times during the day at two p.m. and then at six p.m., and finally before we go to bed at nine-thirty p.m. The simple task of going to the toilet takes most people, what, two to five minutes? Well, for me it is roughly twenty minutes, and that is four times a day.

It is a huge chunk out of my life, especially when you add all the time taken during showering and getting ready for to bed. Who the hell can pee on a time schedule? I don't drink a lot during the day because I don't want to spend the next hour or two needing and waiting to go to the toilet. I don't get to enjoy spending late nights watching movies or writing, because the carers are here at nine-thirty p.m. to put me to bed. I have tried asking the service provider that employs my carers to have them 'on call' for specific times during the day or night, but I have been told that I am not allowed to because of all the red tape.

The service provider has said they need two weeks' notice if we want to go out anywhere. How can one live a life two weeks in advance? You simply can't. What angers me is that they *can* organise carers at a day's notice, and we have to keep reminding them when they forget to put the times on the roster for the days we want to go out. They then complain that we make 'too many changes to the roster' and I feel like I am the bad guy for trying to live a normal life. It is not my fault, and I'd rather not be continually pointing out their mistakes.

Leaving the house is no simple task. We have to pre-plan our whole day just for a couple of hours of being out in the world. I can't stay out for too long because there is nowhere for us to go to the toilet due to the lack of facilities and equipment that we need.

So what happens when the service provider forgets to cover someone's shift? Well, no one turns up. We either lie in bed frustrated as hell, or we sit in our wheelchairs busting to go to the toilet whilst waiting for that second worker to arrive. We have to ring the service provider and wait for them to find someone to come in, if they are available. It may take ten minutes or forty-five minutes. It doesn't matter. We have to wait. This screws our whole day because we can't get that missing time back. We can't simply say, 'Oh, only one carer turned up let's skip going to the toilet today.'

We have the same female carers that return to our home, which is good because it takes time teaching new people the routine, and I don't just let anyone see me naked. In the past we have basically been told to shut up and accept whoever comes through the door and that we should be thankful that we have any care at all. We also have the option of going into an aged care home to get the twenty-four-hour care that we need, but of course our mum was there to make sure things were done right.

A lot has changed since then, and we have carers who are more respectful of our needs, but we still have a long way to go. Having carers come and go every day is extremely hard because they are in our personal lives. We have no privacy of our own. It is also heartbreaking when they move on because sometimes, we don't hear from them again, or if they do keep in contact, it's not the same because we don't see them every day. Meeting new carers is challenging too, because we don't know if they are going to stay or find it too hard and leave without any warning. We have had people say, 'See you tomorrow', but they never return. It is never easy.

Every aspect of our lives is either a struggle to make people understand our situation, or a fight to try to make people see that we *need* the help. We're not asking just because we *want* it. Take our two electric doors at home for an example. We had to pay a couple of thousand dollars for each one because the disability system sees the doors as a luxury. It may be a luxury for some people, but not for us; for Cyanne and I it is about being safe. If we didn't have these electric doors, we wouldn't be able to get out of the house. I can't open a door because I don't have the strength. So how can I get out if there's a fire?

One of the biggest issues I face is not being able to go to the toilet or shower while I am at the hospital. The bathroom facilities are not big enough to fit both a change table and a lifter (this is also the same for every accessible toilet facility in South Australia). I would prefer to keep my modesty and get undressed all in the one room rather than being wheeled naked down the corridor with a sheet wrapped around me. No one would appreciate having to walk naked from room to room to use the toilet or shower. I also have to bring my personal sling, because the standard hospital slings are for much larger people. The toilet chairs are a problem too. They are designed for men and aren't padded—I can't use these chairs because my skinny bum falls through the hole.

Cyanne and I don't like using the taxi service because it is just another thing to organise and to predict what time you need to be picked up and dropped off. I book in advance so they will arrive on time due to the high number of people in wheelchairs using the taxis. We can't even go out together because the taxis only hold one wheelchair, which means that the taxi has to drop one of us off and then go back for the other. We have to pay double for each trip because we both can't fit in one taxi.

One day when Cyanne and I went out, we booked a taxi van. My carer and I arrived at the destination first, and we waited for Cyanne. The taxi driver decided to do another job before picking Cyanne up. We were upset as Cyanne was over an hour late, and it spoiled the whole day. However, on the way back they organised for two taxi vans to pick us up. This surprised us both because I'd last heard they only had one access van. Now they have four! They also have a van that can cater for two wheelchairs, but unfortunately, they didn't have enough seatbelts fitted to use it.

This is just a short view of what it is to be in our world. If we were to fill you in on everything we'd be writing a book. A typical day in our life is very complex, but over the years, it has become second nature to us.

About us

Many people see us as one person because we are twins, but we are two completely individual people. When I am out with my carer I often get asked, 'where is Cyanne?' Sometimes they jump to the conclusion that she is unwell because she is not with me. Sure, we may go to the Council, Youth Advisory Committee (YAC) and Disability Advisory Group meetings, and sometimes to the shops together, but we also have our different likes and tastes, and our own lives.

I am part of the Whyalla Writers' Group and the Society of Editors (SA). I have just completed studying Certificate IV in Legal Services. In 2016 I received my Certificate IV in Small Business Management with a plan to start my own editing and proofreading business called Wondrous Words with Zia. I also have an Advanced Diploma in Arts (Professional Writing), a Certificate in Professional Editing and Proofreading, as well as a Society of Editors (SA) Award for Highest Achievement in Editing.

Cyanne is a member of the Whyalla Access Group and has a Certificate IV in Residential Drafting. She has just received a Diploma in Interior Design and Decoration. On Mondays Cyanne attends the local art gallery to draw with other artists and to share ideas and techniques. She couldn't study art at the university or TAFE campus, as they didn't offer the courses internally or externally. Cyanne is still hoping for an opportunity to enrol in an art class.

But we do have our shared passions and occasionally join forces.

When the Youth Advisory Committee (YAC) organised the International Day for People with Disabilities down at the beach last year (2017), we had also organised Push Mobility to come to the beach to demonstrate the use of the beach mats.

Being able to get down to the beach was amazing. It had been too long since we had been able to get onto the sand, and I can just imagine how many other people are in the same boat. It was an emotional time for us. I think the last time I was able to get onto the sand was when I was about ten years old. I'm now twenty-six. After that Cyanne and I applied for funding through the state government's Fund My Neighbourhood program in 2017 but sadly nothing came of it.

I am working hard to get a Changing Place for Whyalla. A Changing Place is for people with disabilities who require both a hoist and a change table to be dressed and undressed when going to the toilet. You would be surprised at how many people need this facility, and at how often they miss out on events and social outings because of this lack. Until these facilities are available I am limited as to how long I can be out for. Surely it should be the right of those who need it, to be able to access a public toilet with a Changing Place?

What if we were to take away all the public toilets? I am sure there would be many protests, but what about those who cannot use the public toilets because of the lack of room and equipment? You do not see these people out very much because they are at home where the toilet is.

Will we ever give up? Not likely. Cyanne and I have gotten through a tough life so far with our positive attitudes, sense of humour and the belief that we can prompt the changes needed to improve our lives, and the lives of others who face the same problems. Are we strong enough? Take a look at our mum, and I think you might find the answer!

Additional Information:

Facebook media release excerpt August 2017

On August 28th, 2017, Dignity Party MP Kelly Vincent was pleased to announce that thanks to funding secured by Dignity Party SA, the first six Changing Places will be located at Rundle Mall, Glenelg, U City

Franklin Street, and Adelaide Oval, as well as funding for 2 portable Changing Places known as Marveloos.

Excerpt from the *Whyalla News* 24-1-2018

Access to the beach for those who use a wheelchair will now be much easier thanks to a beach access mat being funded by the state government.

Local twins Zia and Cyanne Westerman campaigned tirelessly for the mat, submitting their idea to the state government's Fund My Neighbourhood program in 2017.

The idea did not get funded through that program but has now been given the full funding of $37,000 from the state government.

Facebook media release excerpt from 1st February 2018

The Dignity Party are incredibly pleased to announce Cyanne Westerman - Dignity Party candidate for Giles.

On the same day as her launch by Dignity Party Leader Kelly Vincent, Cyanne Westerman had a win lobbying for changing places in regional SA.

NINETEEN

Bee-Longing

by Bee Williamson

When you feel you belong, you do. Nobody needs to tell you.

I remember what that feels like. I was fourteen. My mum and I had moved from Melbourne to the green hinterland of Byron Shire, and I had just started at a new school, Mullumbimby High.

On one of those days that began with awkwardness and eating lunch alone in the library, a girl came to see me. She asked my name and had I once been at Middle Park Primary?

'Emily!'

'Yes,' she said. 'We were friends in second grade. Boy, you've blossomed.'

At that moment we became friends again. Emily was funny and eccentric. We teamed up with a lovely, tall and very funny friend Tara, and became inseparable.

These were the belonging years. Theatre, dance, singing in extra-curricular community theatre, school productions, competing in theatre-sports, bold raids on the beer fridge at the Old Drill Hall. Late night explorations of this little town and its local newspaper's cameras– anything to bring a rush.

non-belonging

When we came to Australia, I was the youngest of three kids. We all went to Middle Park Primary.

At first, I was called a 'Pommy bastard' and resorted to counting stickers on the walls of the school. I think my Obsessive-Compulsive Disorder (OCD) may have started then. After a while, I had a few friends. In fourth grade, a girl turned against me, and turned the whole grade against me as well. I don't know what I did or said, but I know I never dressed right. Never in Esprit or Sportsgirl. My hair wasn't cut right either. I think I was still getting my mum to cut my hair until I was twenty! We were poor.

That's where the library lunches started. I learnt the Dewey system and helped the librarians sort the books and tidy the shelves and take the cards. Then in grade six, I became one of the misfits. I was friends with the freaks: the 'fat' one, the hairy one, the one who pees under desks, and me, the weird one, who plaits her hair and wears a trench coat. One girl called me the 'Grim Reaper'.

Where were my stepbrothers during this time? We didn't get on, so I imagine I didn't think to ask them to take my side in the school ground. *Kids can be cruel,* they say. Out of school, I was also fearful: I was often followed to school by men in trucks and cars, on bicycles and motorbikes. Eventually, my folks got me a green pushbike. I was so relieved.

much needed friendship
During these hard years at school, I had a good friend. She saved me from the nightmare of middle-class rot. Her name was Kelly. Her father ran a café...a reggae café! On the weekends we would make hot chocolates for the punters...my step-mum would read her poetry on their poetry nights. I grew up going to all the local haunts, the Provincial, the Perseverance...The next morning, Kelly and I would dance and muck around; we had the whole space to ourselves, and we would dance to Bob Marley and the Wailers. We would have Picnic bars and Snickers for breakfast! No one told us off, and no one put us in our place. We were free. And in these years I discovered my love of dance. It freed me, as Kelly's friendship did.

We used to foot-fight and got quite rough. Upstairs, up above the café, were two levels and a roof garden. Kelly and I would dress up and try on the stilettos that were in every colour of the rainbow. We would dress up most nights. Kelly had long wavy brown hair down to her waist. I remember it used to take an hour to blow-wave dry. Past the tiny kitchen was the rooftop garden. Up there, we slept on the trampoline under the stars. I would fall asleep wondering about the rumours that someone 'roof-jumped' with a crate and rope, along the other roofs. We were kids, and free enough to be real kids.

philosophy and tea
Much later, when I went to stay in Byron Bay during my college breaks, I stayed with Gilli, my step-mum. Days were spent swimming, reading but mostly talking, sipping tea and smoking rollies. Gilli was a highly-educated and emotional woman with feminist leanings. We spent hours talking about philosophy, relationships and Simone de Beauvoir. We connected over the

troublesome issues of family, and in this way, I felt a true sense of belonging. For the first time, I wasn't considered mad for all my feelings and intuitions. I was finally able to fit into my extended family and enjoy philosophy and tea.

sunroom jams

When I moved to Elwood, I followed a new friend, and a new circle of her friends suddenly became my new normal. I had gone for the big UK trip in 1998 and came back and got very sick with glandular fever. A year or so before, I also got three tick bites that weren't properly removed and so I developed chronic fatigue. Many afternoons were spent sipping herbal tea and playing guitars in the sunroom with my new friends.

I wanted it to last forever, but eventually, I moved to Carlton and very little of 'true' was left of the friendships. Is such a full sense of belonging worth the regret when it's gone? By the time my schizophrenia hit, very few of my old friends knew how to talk to the mania and depression.

owls at 4 am

When I told a studio mate that I was writing a piece on belonging, he went quiet for a moment and then said, 'Blimey'. He had a Scottish name and he told me of its provenance and a famous man in a famous battle. My father's name always linked me with pride. Grandad was a famous English writer and naturalist, often called the 'Last Romantic'. His work is taught in schools still. His name was associated with owls and for a long time, I would receive owls as gifts, of metal, fur, feather, wood, fabric, glass and clay. I was owl-mad. I was proud my family totem was a barn owl, as I was first introduced to one when I was four years old, during the middle of the night. I remember they had such delicate, white, snowy wings.

Now my grandfather's spirit no longer watches over me, and the owl trinkets have slowed. He has moved on to a new life.

And so have I.

diagnosis: chronic

Within the first six months of a person getting sick, they wait this time out to see what your diagnosis is, and after six months my psychiatrist said I had schizophrenia. I was initially sceptical, and so were my parents. Separated when I was four years of age, they both were close to me, living in the same city, just a few minutes' drive to each other. Initially my mum was left in England, while we all moved to Melbourne. Neither of them believed my diagnosis; I think this was because the onset was so sudden and out of the blue. In just one week I went from functioning and healthy, to psychotic, to mute, catatonic and posturing. So it is understandable they didn't want me on heavy antipsychotics.

I fought for my life the whole year after I was diagnosed, coming on and off my medications. I tried quite a few different anti-psychotics, but none of them really worked. I was told that I was kept off my gold standard pill because I was a young woman and therefore wouldn't want to be overweight. I was angered by this.

I had a year of psychosis that my new pills could have fixed. I got my life back in September 2002 when they finally put me on Olanzapine. Now I had my sanity back. I eventually went back to part-time work as a graphic designer and started exhibiting my artworks, including photography. I have now been part of twenty-six exhibitions. I lost that time after diagnosis because they didn't want me to get fat. I say, 'I'd rather be fat and sane, than skinny and mad!'

dancing nights

Before my diagnosis, when I was at college, I lived with several girlfriends in a run-down seven-bedroom dilapidated mansion on the beach in St Kilda we called Mazza Pazza. We had wild nights of parties and birthdays. Nights of belly dancing circles and massage circles, chanting evenings and vegetarian feasts.

They were wild times! Wild parties full of outrageously-costumed women and guys. But it was what I needed. I loved 'bed-hopping' with my new and old girlfriends. Some would snore, and one even used to sit bolt upright and talk to herself in her sleep. Our beds had satin sheets, sheepskins on the floor and lace curtains draped around the windows ... lots of feathers on the walls, with murals in the kitchen. We had a filthy, run-down bath outside that I loved! We would clean it, but it was so old you couldn't tell.

At college, I was very shy, but I knew I had really good friends at home, so I was always relieved to get home, where I could have someone to talk to. I didn't tell my friends at home that I was so unhappy at uni, being too shy to talk to friends there ... my fear of blushing was a big issue. But, belonging to the 'Mazza Pazza' women, with their silk dresses and feathers and beads in their hair, glitter masks and feasts of roast veggies, rice and soya mayo - those days were blessed.

Nilgun and blue satin dolls

I joined Rag Theatre in 2006, while Nilgun Guven was the director. Nilgun turned out to be the best director I'd ever had! I'd met her through a local women's show that we did with Sally-Anne Upton. Called 'Swimming in my Head', it was a great community gig for women. I approached the group with some writing I'd done during an episode a few years prior. I wasn't sure of the piece, but I got a great response. It was an incredibly raw and revealing monologue.

I performed it during our season at Theatreworks. After the final show, I stepped out into the foyer ... suddenly people kept coming up to me and saying how wonderful my monologue was. I got feedback that night that I had never received before! The piece was dead honest with a lot of self-loathing. Apparently, this resonated with the audience, because they were coming up to me one after the other. One said it was the best theatre they'd seen, and what 'real theatre should be'.

My sense of belonging was fulfilled again because of Nilgun and these shows we did this year.

loves you, warts and all

I have been in therapy since 2005, and my psychologist has shown such care in my mental health. With the number of issues I bombard her with, most would walk away. But she has loved and cared for me, in all the bleak times. Like when I cried my way, walking to her home, and said I thought I was the devil. How do people deal with that? How can she listen, month after month? Of course the money helps! But she really is my own Yoda: my own emerald Buddha, sitting, with eyes twinkling, saying, 'You're worthy of love'. How she can hear the things I say and not kick me out her door, I do not know?! Sometimes I think back and wonder, 'Did I actually say that?' My own loving, emerald Buddha loves me, warts and all.

just being there

When my mum opens her arms, I just fold into her. Just her presence, her warm demure face, etched in sadness, is all I need to love. She has given me the greatest gift—a life. And now, with schizo-affective disorder, she has had to walk the line that is mother and carer to me, her adult daughter. Without a mother's love, I really don't know how my sick fellows travel in life.

I am sitting in my big studio, in St Kilda, quite happy on my own. I have music, coffee and a little chocolate. I am happy writing, designing and making art. But I go home to her. Yes, I have a real home that I am happy to return to. But so many in my situation do not have any of these things. Mental illness can preclude having any of these stabilities, and leave the vulnerable, especially the elderly, homeless. Mum may think she didn't give me enough strength to live properly, but I did learn the skills to get by, like saving money and paying rent on time, committing to work and giving my all to creative projects. I may have to get taxis instead of public transport, but that is minor in the scheme of things.

just belonging

Just belonging is such a rich and beautiful feeling. But, in life, feelings change, shift, grow, or dissolve. The feelings can last in activities like theatre and deepen in pure friendship. These may last or maybe not. Now I am involved in a mental health website where I am a peer support advisor. I have found friendships and discussions there that rival a $270 session with a private psychiatrist!

the most hated woman to walk on Earth

What I know now is not what I knew then. There was a moment in my deep depression and chronic OCD that developed alongside schizo-affective disorder, when I felt I was the most hated woman on earth. It was probably a voice that said that to me, while I walked to the shops one morning. And, do you know, I believed it was true? I felt the intrusive thoughts of harming others had made me into a monster. Yet they were 'just thoughts' as my psychologist said. When you have OCD thoughts, you are not yourself. Not your inner, true, meaningful self. If you could look inside my mind then, you would see a disaster. I just hung on to the idea that I was actually a peaceful, caring person, as my family around me kept reminding me.

And, I learnt not to identify with my thoughts. We walk around thinking, and thinking defines us, it is who we are. But I had to learn that I wasn't my thoughts ... they didn't make me who I was. I had to resonate with a deeper, calmer, wordless self. This brought me to Eckhart Tolle's meditation technique. I use full body meditation, lying down, for many hours at a time. It has helped me cope with chronic back pain and clear illness after surgery. It has kept me out of the psych wards. It has kept me just walking the dog, day after day, around the same streets for thirteen years – every time a joy. If you have thoughts you are scared of, see someone, and know, you are not your thoughts, you are much, much more.

TWENTY

How to Be Beautiful
by Grant Lock

I WAS THE DIRECTOR OF AFGHANISTAN'S LARGEST EYE-CARE program ... then came the shock.

'Rest your chin on the guide, Mr Lock, and look straight ahead.' On the other side of the instrument, my ophthalmologist lowers his head and peers. He mumbles something and straightens up. He frowns, 'It's Stargardt's Disease.' My mind is racing. *Stargardt's disease! What a terrible name. It must be something awful. What started it? Was it our twenty years in Pakistan? The grit and the glare of digging wells in the desert? Or building schools and hospitals on the Afghan border? The monsoon? The flies? The disease? Or in Afghanistan the constant travelling to visit eye-hospitals? Dust storms? Snow-glare? Could that have started it?*

The specialist is reading my thoughts. 'It's nothing to do with where you have worked.' He pauses, 'It's genetic. In fact, you've been lucky.'

I feel my eyebrows coming together. *Lucky? What is this guy talking about? Lucky? How can that be?*

'Yes,' he says, 'Very lucky. It is also called Juvenile Onset Macular Degeneration. Most people with this lose their central vision before they reach ten or twenty years of age.'

I'm stunned. I knew that something was going wrong with my vision. Difficulty reading in poor light. Losing sight of the volleyball when it was falling towards me. And cars coming out of nowhere on the Kabul roads. *I'm just getting older*, I thought, *I just need a new pair of glasses. But now this ... this Stargardt's thing. I'm going blind ... and he says I'm lucky!*

'Hold on Grant,' a small voice says inside me, 'Didn't he just say it should have happened when you were a teenager? You've had a forty-five year extension. How good is that!' I start to smile, well, at least half-smile. Forty-five years? Pretty good I reckon. I lean back. A multitude of images video across my brain. The stud beef cattle breeding. The tennis courts. The ballroom dancing. The cross-cultural training. The Afghan widows my wife mentored. My three kids at sports days in Pakistan. The confrontation with bearded men with guns, when building a girls' school. And the great team of foreign volunteers and enthusiastic locals in Afghanistan. Hiking above the snow-line. Snorkelling in Bali.

Out of the haze, I hear the doctor speaking. 'It will rapidly get worse. You will have to leave Afghanistan.' Then he answered my next unspoken question. 'Hard to tell,' he says, 'there is no treatment. You have to leave Afghanistan immediately. And don't forget to hand in your driver's license. Soon you won't be able to read at all.'

In 2008, my gutsy wife, the one the Kabul widows called 'Farishta' (angel), and I, returned to Australia. 'Hardly a fair deal,' one of my mates says, 'You were out there for twenty-four years, end up being director of that huge eye-care program, then you go blind yourself.' He doesn't have to articulate further. He knows I am a person of faith and I know he is thinking: 'What kind of God is that?'

But I like to focus on the positives. Those extra forty-five years of central vision. The opportunity to see lives changed, to see kids going to school. To see widows earn a living. To see remote villages, connected to micro-hydro power. To see sight restored to the old and the young. To plan, laugh, cry and work hard with a great team. To sit on the floor, and eat hot naan-bread with the locals. And I am thankful too for the technology which now allows me to write my books poetry and short stories.

And yes, I have become more and more empathetic with those who are marginalised by some disability. Whether it is with faulty eyes, like me, or deafness, or PTSD, or a wheelchair. Or maybe as a newcomer to our country, wearing different clothes, and not very good at English.

So now I am going to tell you how to be beautiful.

> I used to be the one who looked out for the loner,
> but now....
> after the meeting
> it's time for tea,
> mix and match,
> laugh and chat.
> But as for me
> I'm out of community.
> Dysfunction at the junction
> where personality and disability

meet gut-level grief and pain.
I peer at you,
my faceless friends,
in vain.
There's a fuzzy wall
between me and you.
Lonely corner,
bitter pie.
No Jack. No Horner.
Alone am I.
These fractured molecules
in a seemingly functional cell.
I feel unneeded,
useless,
redundant.
Macular slice of separation.
The taste of hell.
Leper.
'Unclean. Unclean.'
Can't you hear my bell
ringing out the warning?
Yet pleading for your touch,
your voice,
your association.
Surely that's not too much to ask!
But here I float,
below the bastions of your castles,
melting iceberg in a lonely moat.
And in this opaque corner,
marginalised by the unseeing focus
of my muddy eyes,

internally I scream,
'Where are you, Jack?
Where are you, Horner?'
Mrs Glibly passes by.
'Er, who are you?'
I tentatively ask.
Glibly she replies,
'But Grant! You know me!
You know my voice!'
And glibly
she swans into the night.
But I have no choice,
if I can't make the connection right.
I'm lost,
alone,
out in the cold.
Old Jack Frost.
Then,
out of the audio forest,
you come,
a welcome, blurry tree.
I feel your touch,
I hear my name.
You say, 'Grant, come and join us.
Come with me!'
Thank you.
You are beautiful.
Grant Lock 2016

Grant Lock is the author of two popular books. *Shoot Me First: a cattleman in Taliban country. Twenty-four years in the hotspots of Pakistan and Afghanistan*, and *I'd Rather Be Blind: The night hides a world but reveals a universe. My life after Afghanistan.*

Both are available at bookshops and on Amazon and Book Depository. *Shoot Me First* is also available in audio form. Grant is a popular motivating speaker, story-teller, and poet.

Email: grantlock@shootmefirst.com

TWENTY-ONE

A Treasure Hunter

by Alex Blackmore and Nadja Fernandes

ONCE I HEARD A PHRASE THAT STUCK IN MY HEAD: 'NATURE never allows a man to be more than what he is, only less'.[15] Recently, I have been pondering about that quote even more intensely, after having been acquainted with someone I've come to consider spectacular.

Eight years ago, in a small town in the outback of the state of South Australia, Aaron and Lauren were expecting their second child. Another boy, named Alex, was on his way. He was destined to be a very, very special one.

Today, it's a busy household, with four children aged ten, eight, four and one: Elliott, Alex, Betty and Sophie, respectively. There's also a four-year-old Chihuahua, whom Alex named 'Shortie', after a character from an *Indiana Jones* movie—which is quite an irony,

---

15 From Netflix series, *The Alienist*. Accessed March 18 2019.

since the character himself is believed to have been named after a pet dog. Then there is a budgie—as if there was any need for more noise in the house—and a fish called 'Super Blue'. There used to be two fish, but rumour has it that Super Blue was so hungry that one day he simply ate his girlfriend. But that didn't upset Alex. He already had a good notion about the food chain system and about 'surviving', even though that was a bit before he got hooked on the TV show *Survivor*.

Alex was born with Spina Bifida, a congenital malformation in which there is an incomplete closing of the backbone and also the membranes around the backbone. That means that the spine does not develop in the expected way and each vertebra looks like a bite has been taken out of it. The main implication is that Alex was born paraplegic and as such, would never able to walk on his own. Still, he loves sport and is a bright, active and happy child.

As I'm speaking on the phone to his mum, Lauren, I hear a lot of noise in the background. So much noise that she has to excuse herself for a moment to go and get the level down. This is part of what I hear:

> ... Well, why don't you let her have that ball and get the other one?
> ... I don't want the other one.
> ... Well, there are three balls, and you are three children. There is one for each of you.

A few more words of wisdom from a very calm, loving and skilful mum, and peace is re-established among Elliott, Alex and Betty. We continue our conversation, and I can't help wishing I had her skills. Meanwhile, my daughter is singing loudly in the living room. I just keep my bedroom door closed and hope that she stays as far away as possible for the duration of my phone conversation, so I don't have to put my own skills to the test. It either worked, or Lauren was too polite to let me know otherwise.

Like many children, Alex started school at the age of five. There he befriended a girl called Abigail, who was in his classroom, and the pair became inseparable. Soon it was established they were ... an 'item'. One morning, two years down the track, the two of them were swimming. Abigail got out of the pool first, and Alex followed. As she watched him crawling, she inquired, 'Why don't you get up and walk rather than crawl?' Her mother interfered and replied, 'Abigail! He can't'. That was when Abigail became aware that Alex was not able to walk. It seems that the two years they had shared were so occupied with other activities they both took part in, that Alex's inability to walk was just a minor detail, so insignificant that it literally went unnoticed by the seven-year-old girl.

They're still in touch regularly, although Alex and his family have moved from Andamooka to Adelaide. Nevertheless, they meet at least once a year. In addition to that, they Skype and exchange emails quite often and are both very much aware of what is going on in each other's lives.

Contrary to what some might imagine due to his physical condition, Alex is extremely active. Physical education is one of his two favourite subjects at school. Swimming is his number one favourite sport, and he has been swimming for a number of years. In 2017 he joined a local Wheelchair Australian Football team and was an active player in the competition. Although his team did not do really well, he is very proud to tell us, with his great sense of humour, that his team came last! It wasn't as easy to accept during the final game, when his dad had to fill in because they were one player short. During the match, Alex was heard saying in quite a loud voice, 'Dad, stop it. You are the loser!' With a competitive nature, Alex had to leave the court for a few minutes to compose himself. After the game, Alex approached his dad and informed him, 'Dad, you made us lose'. Alex knew his team only lost that game because his dad seemed to be such an unskilled player, but Alex got over the defeat in no time. Well done, Alex! He is also a member of the local Cub Scouts and absolutely loves outdoor activities, having recently won a first-place ribbon at a sports day. Have I mentioned he also goes surfing? He got a trophy for 'Best Wipeout' at a competition organised by the Disabled Surfers Association of Australia. Apparently, he crashed off a wave and fell, getting his face covered in sand. The association has professional surf trainers for the disabled, and Alex's dad, who's an experienced surfer, approached one of them to get some help so he'd be better equipped to train Alex.

> Q: What do you miss most about Andamooka?
> A: Camping all the time, fishing, and going yabbying. And living next door to Grandpa.
> Q: What's so special about him? - I ask, with curiosity.
> A: Oh, he's a bit silly. And great fun.

Then to make his point he tells me that not that long ago they were all expecting a visit from his grandfather, and when he arrived, it was not the grandfather his sister Betty expected. She looked disappointed and said, 'I want the other grandfather'. It just so happens that the 'silly grandfather', aka *Ratbag*, had already won little Betty over. Having said that, the other granddad had no trouble showing he was also cool in his own way, and soon enough, Betty no longer requested the Ratbag's presence.

Alex's grandfather—yes, Ratbag—was an opal miner and occasionally still takes the boys into escapades underground, which is why Alex has a jar full of opal chips. I see a photo of an impressive rock with a prominent blue vein of crystal opal, which I am told is the best sort. I am also reminded that it was Alex himself who found it, digging through the dirt that others had missed.

All that love for outdoor activities doesn't mean he can't appreciate a good video game. In fact, he is hoping to be given a PlayStation 4 for his birthday, which is at the beginning of June. At the moment, his favourite game is called *Fortnite*, a game in which multiple players jump out of a plane onto an island, and each must fight for their own survival, hiding from different types of danger. I knew nothing about the game until I looked it up. It comes as no surprise that Alex is enjoying this game so much, given his love of *Survivor*.

Alex is quite fond of fast food, especially pizza, although it seems that not any pizza will do. Take away? No, sir! Mummy's pizza seems to be the winner. After I found that out, I started to wish I could try Lauren's homemade pizza. It must be really good if he says that it is second to none. As for sugar, he also has a sweet tooth. It's been two weeks since Easter and I've heard he's the only one who has been able to stretch his Easter eggs, with two bunnies still intact. That reminds me of another fact about Alex: he is also very fond of bees—has that got anything to do with the honey, I wonder–and he has expressed the wish to have a beehive at home, but his parents aren't quite convinced yet. The compromise is that they're visiting the zoo soon, as there is an active beehive on display at the moment in the Adelaide Zoo.

How does Alex spend his days? Not very different from the ordinary child, with the exception of a couple of things. In the morning, he is assisted with intimate personal care, which takes about an hour, and generally happens around 6.40 a.m. After this, he showers—and I'm told he has a very independent nature, so he showers by himself—dresses, watches some cartoons, has something to eat and wheels to school with his big brother, Elliott. I am told Alex is a popular kid at school, and really enjoys maths—although not as much as phys-ed. He also likes Greek, his LOTE (Language other than English) subject. So would I, if my foreign language teacher was such a cool lady, part of a music band. I wonder if she had any part in Alex's appreciation for music. He has recently taken up the guitar, and can sometimes be heard playing *Peter Gunn*, music by *Queen* and the theme song of *Mission Impossible*.

Alex leads quite a busy life. Every night he has a different sport or plays cards. Some days he has 'Conductive Education', which I've recently learned is a Hungarian hands-on therapy method that consists of training people with motor disorders with the view to reducing their dependence on artificial aids and enabling them to become more independent. I've been told it also helps Alex with his general blood circulation and muscle functions, and it's good for his overall well-being. Alex does that twice a week.

Very fond of sleeping in, Alex sleeps between eight to ten hours every night. He definitely does not like getting out of bed, which accounts for his high appreciation of holiday time. Much as he likes school, he has no hesitation in telling me he prefers being on holidays.

As I hear more about this boy, I feel almost as if I've known him for longer. *I wonder why?* I ask myself silently until I find out that Alex, as well as digging for opals, enjoys going to garage sales. He has a fine eye for good findings—another type of treasure—his latest being an old typewriter, which he's been using to write movie reviews. This is the opening of one of his reviews: 'A long time ago in a galaxy far, far away'. Any guesses? You got it. He's reviewing all the *Star War* movies. I feel embarrassed to admit I have never seen any but am resolved to watching at least one now that I know of his fondness. I look at the photo of this gorgeous, bespectacled lad, sitting at the table behind a typewriter, with a glass of water on his left and a mug on the right—a Milo perhaps? I am not sure, but I do know that if I had met him when I was in primary school, it would probably have been love at first sight. Have I mentioned Clark Kent was my first crush? I was fascinated by the glasses AND the typing. So I understand his girlfriend's interest. What great taste she has! From what I hear, I think their relationship is quite stable. The only problem I see is how they are going to solve a minor dispute: Alex wants to have two children, but Abigail wants twelve! Perhaps one day she'll manage to explain to him what the expression 'cheaper by the dozen' means … And I can't wait to read his review on that movie.

TWENTY-TWO

Daring to Dream
by Mary Albury and Valerie Everett

IF THERE WAS ONE WISH GRANTED TO ME RIGHT NOW, I KNOW exactly what it would be. That my beloved mum could see everything I accomplished in my life. From the day I was born, she had dreams for me, and I am proud to say I have achieved every one. At first glance, her list of dreams would seem fairly straightforward: to discover life's wonders, experience new things, meet someone special to share my life with, and seek knowledge in order to make a difference. In a few plain words: to live a fulfilled life.

It is fair to say that my mum's dreams for me were similar to what most parents have for their children. Yet, I was not like most children. The odds of my success were stacked against me from the very day I entered the world. I had a severe disability, and the doctor's prognosis for my life was bleak. However, on my life's journey, I am living proof that negative expectations at birth are not necessarily an accurate prediction of how one's life can unfold.

My name is Mary Albury, and I was born in Brisbane on 3 July 1980 by Caesarean section. I came a day early and in distress; a limp, blue and lifeless baby caused by oxygen deprivation as the umbilical cord was wrapped around my neck. By the age of three, I was diagnosed with Cerebral Palsy, and medical experts were not optimistic about my future. When my mum was advised that I was not expected to talk, walk, sit or eat without assistance, she refused to accept a word of it. Instead, she wanted me to have the best life possible and set the bar high in terms of the dreams and hopes she had for me.

From the start, my mum steered my life with her positive and proactive attitude. At the same time that she was hearing my adverse prognosis, she was supporting me to develop some independence. At the age of three, I was given my first power wheelchair, which enabled my freedom. It was hot pink and, at the time, I was the youngest child in Queensland to have one. My mum supported my schooling from an early age. I attended the special school attached to the Cerebral Palsy League of Queensland, in New Farm, an inner-city suburb of Brisbane, and there I received intensive therapies that helped me throughout the school day. To my delight, I got to spend time with a young boy called Byron, who had a beaming smile. He also had a wheelchair, although his was not hot pink! Byron always made me feel safe, looked out for me and encouraged me to work harder with my physical endeavours. He was my first real friend.

My mum was also my biggest supporter, and 'my rock' during medical treatments in my early years. I endured countless hours of painful and often frustrating medical treatments: physiotherapy, occupational therapy and speech pathology. Through it all, she was always by my side.

At home, Mum was determined that my life would be 'typical' as I was growing up. I was expected to do chores and participate fully in family life. With my mum's encouragement and support, I achieved every developmental milestone of a child my age. Additionally, she was deeply aware of my educational ability and needs. By the age of six, she realised that the special school no longer provided me with sufficient intellectual stimulation and, subsequently, I was sent to a mainstream school.

My mum and I shared a special bond. I was always her daughter first, and my disability came second. When I wasn't at school or in therapy, we spent many precious hours together: shopping, driving to the beach or just relaxing on the couch watching a romantic comedy. Her support, encouragement and love were unconditional. She was my saving grace, and I could not imagine living without her. But, unexpectedly, my life was to change drastically.

I began high school at St Thomas More College in Sunnybank, a southern suburb of Brisbane, but in Year Eight, some nine days after my fourteenth birthday, my world was shattered. Tragically, my wonderful mum passed away, just when I needed her the most. In addition to Cerebral Palsy, I had been diagnosed with scoliosis as a young child, and with the onset of puberty, it had worsened. Now, I could barely sit up and was only breathing effectively through one lung. It was debilitating, and I required complex spinal surgery—an operation that my mum had previously promised to be by my side for, if it was ever necessary. The night before my surgery, my fright and panic were indescribable. My only glimmer of hope, sad as it may sound, was that if the operation failed and I passed away, then at least I would have been reunited with my mum!

Thankfully, I wasn't on my own; my wonderful family and in particular, my grandmother, reassured me that I would never have to face the world alone, even if it meant them putting their own lives and needs on hold. My family, friends and a supportive school community rallied around me, not only to ensure that I could remain at home after the operation; they kept Mum's vision for my life alive and moving forward. Their selflessness, compassion and patience gave me the strength to slowly emerge from the fog of my sadness and, in time, learn how to smile and see life as precious and meaningful, once more.

It was also around the time of my mum's passing that I realised, with her gone, I needed to grow up faster and learn the skills of personal advocacy. I needed to help my family to understand my routines and the best ways to respond to my changing needs. I had to become an expert in my own care and be able to communicate this knowledge to others, so they could adequately provide the support I needed.

My operation went ahead in November 1994, and when I awoke, the eighty-six external staples that held my incisions together let me know I was alive! Every single muscle in my body felt it had been stretched like a strand of homemade spaghetti. Each day of my recovery presented new challenges, and I sought solace by visiting the nursery adjacent to my room. There, I rocked the adorable newborn babies and came to an amazing realisation. My operation must have been successful as already I was reaping benefits! I was rocking these little bundles in their cots all by myself. I had a straight spine that could now support my body. I was becoming stronger and could now drive my wheelchair in a more upright position that gave me a significantly better view of the world. My life was changing, and I was beginning to discover life's wonders. Just as my mum had hoped.

It wasn't all joyful, as institutionalised care came next and the following month was the longest in my life. I received expert care, but being away from my family was heartbreaking, and the monotony of the exercises was almost more than I could bear. My days started early, and I endured endless exercises and hydrotherapy, collapsing into bed each night, grateful that the ordeal had ended. Even then, I could only stay in the one position for two hours before I needed to be rolled again into another position. Finally, I was allowed to go home, three days before Christmas and grateful for everything that was done for me.

After Christmas and the New Year break, I returned to Year Nine at the high school and I was the first student in a wheelchair to be integrated into the mainstream classroom. I socialised with friends while building my own resilience against negative attitudes, and at times, the scourge of bullying. My schooling ran smoothly until I entered my senior year when I realised that something was wrong. I was having multiple epileptic seizures that were scary and debilitating, causing me to lose my vision, speech and ability to move.

After months of testing, I was diagnosed with pseudo-epilepsy, and the cause was pinpointed as stress. Counselling and medication were deemed the answers and, with them, I was able to continue at school, although my health and mental issues severely impacted on my ability to achieve. I graduated from Year Twelve, and was proud to be presented with the 'Personal Growth Award' at the graduation ceremony, in recognition of my resilience and ability to succeed despite adversity.

After Year Twelve, I wanted to pursue further education—another of my mum's dreams that I would seek knowledge to make a difference. Consequently, I commenced an Arts degree, majoring in journalism, hoping to use my gift of writing skills to make a difference in the world. I wasn't quite sure how I would achieve that outcome when I began the course.

At the same time, there was another direction I wanted to take. Perhaps it was my mum's dream that I experience new things, that motivated me to take up a number of voluntary roles. These included occasional child-minding, including a vacation care program for children with disabilities and their siblings. I also wanted to 'do my bit' for the advocacy movement for people with disabilities. To that end, I was appointed the Chairperson of the Regional Client Consultative Committee that met regularly at a supported employment service located in Tingalpa. The committee covered a wide region, south of the Brisbane River, and all the way to the Gold Coast. The committee's goals included improving the forum for open discussion and debate so that service delivery within the Cerebral Palsy League could be improved and more responsive. My role as chairperson was to facilitate discussion about issues that were being experienced across the region and draw on common experiences. Our committee's yearly planning day required us to collaborate with our counterparts from the state arm of the committee, and it was at one of our meetings where, to my delight, I was reacquainted with an old friend from my past. It was Byron, the boy with the beaming smile and great personality, whom I had met at the special school fifteen years before. He was the Chairperson of the State Client Consultative Committee for Queensland!

We began a four-year courtship of dating, dinners, dancing and movies. We had the best time ever, although sometimes in the face of unexpected negativity and occasionally, outright rudeness. He was, and still is, a wheelchair-user and occasionally, when other people saw us together, perhaps at dinner, they would comment rudely or stare and gawk unnecessarily. We felt like animals in a zoo!

On one occasion, a couple eating dinner next to us got up and moved away. Another time, Byron was helping me finish a meal by scooping the last of the food onto my fork and placing it in my mouth, when a diner asked bluntly, 'Must you do that here?'—perhaps asserting that our presence and behaviour in the restaurant were inappropriate. Such reactions make me wish that, in this day and age, we could go out like every other couple without someone feeling the need to stare or feel sorry for us. People need to know this. We don't feel sorry for our predicament and are just going about our business, enjoying life like everybody else.

It was around this time that I left university and quit my Arts Degree. After six years my heart just wasn't in it, but I retained my passion for writing. I felt so strongly about my disability and how I was being treated by the community that, at the age of twenty-six, I wrote and self-funded the publication of my life story *Who's Been Sitting in My Chair?* Writing it was therapeutic in itself and the fulfilment of a childhood dream. Ambitiously, I published 400 copies that were distributed mainly by word of mouth, while others I gave away, believing they would be an educational tool for people to be inspired by reading my story. Overwhelmingly, the reaction to the honest and candid account of my life was positive. Readers commented that once they began reading, they had trouble putting the book down, which I interpreted as affirmation. My decision to tell my story was right!

By 2004, another of my mum's wishes for me came true when Byron proposed, and I accepted. To my great joy, we were engaged, and I had found that someone special with whom to share my life. Yet, his proposal reminded me of something I had said to my mum when I was a little girl. I told her that I would not get married until

I could walk down the aisle! I was determined to do it, but it meant setting myself a goal that required a degree of determination I had never before faced.

For me to walk meant a year filled with a rigorous program of two hydro-therapy sessions and three hour-long physiotherapy sessions per week. It was sweat-inducing, muscle-hurting hard work, but as far as I was concerned, the pain just made it more worthwhile. Eventually, I was getting stronger, and with the help of a very expensive walker, I started taking my very first independent steps. It was incredible! My steps increased until I could eventually take daily walks around the block. Something I had never done before!

Meanwhile, our wedding plans continued and, once again, I was at times devastated by the attitudes of people. Sometimes business owners would pass negative judgements and question outright my decision to get married, perhaps asking, 'Do you know what love is?' or 'Can you afford this item?' Such views were disheartening, but in no way did they challenge my intention to live my own life as I wished.

Finally, after a year of wedding planning and my determination to gain physical strength, everything reached fruition in June 2004. I kept reminding myself that some people are lucky enough to meet their heroes and today, I would marry mine. In the taxi, en route to the gardens, I revealed my secret to my father about my intention to 'walk down the aisle'. Just saying it out loud made me very excited and extremely nervous. I knew that I needed every ounce of physical and mental strength to pull off my surprise. I worked towards this for a year, and today was the day. There was no turning back!

When we arrived at the gardens, I left the car and the wedding song I had chosen began to play. Incidentally, the song *Everything*

I do, I do it for you, by Bryan Adams, wasn't selected for romantic reasons—it was the only song long enough to allow me the time I needed to walk down the aisle! When I arose from my wheelchair and began walking it was incredible. Step by step, as I passed my friends and family, I caught glimpses of their expressions. Some were crying while others were aghast with their mouths open in utter disbelief and amazement. At first, many of them thought that I must have been using a mechanical walker, until they saw my feet. Only then did they realise the truth. I was walking! As I kept stepping forward, the reactions of the audience paled in comparison to that of the groom and wedding party. Byron was so surprised and proud of me that he was wiping away tears and willing me towards him. Our service began, and if I thought that walking was going to be the hardest part, I had forgotten about remaining standing for its duration. Everything went absolutely perfectly as we exchanged vows.

My wedding day was the greatest and most special day of my life. I only wish that my mum could have been there to see what I accomplished. I did it! I walked down the aisle when I got married, just as I had declared to her as a little girl.

From that special day forward, our lives have been entwined as a happily married couple. Being a wife has been wonderful, and in June 2018 we celebrated our fourteenth wedding anniversary. There have been challenges, of course! The two of us both need support workers on a daily basis, for personal care and domestic support, which increases complexity in our lives. Our home is not always the sanctuary that other married couples have, as we need to welcome people in at the very times when we most want to be alone. Although grateful for the help received, we often feel that our privacy is being invaded, but we have a solution. We are proactive by sharing the expectations we have of support workers, so that their presence does not interfere with our private lives.

My married life has been wonderful, although I knew that there was still one dream of my mum's that was incomplete. It was still alive in my mind. The dream to seek knowledge in order to make a difference. In 2017, with encouragement from Byron, I returned to university study after a fifteen-year absence and enrolled part-time in the brand-new Bachelor of Counselling offered through Griffith University. I believe that when I complete this course, it will allow me the opportunity to provide counselling and support to people from any walk of life, with or without a disability, to bring about positive change and direction in their lives.

My university study has presented me with more challenges, such as a lack of wheelchair access on campus, but I am passionate about my course and determined to achieve my goal. Aside from mobility challenges, I am delighted to have been accepted as an equal at university which motivates me to persevere with my studies even more. So far my grades have been excellent, and I am hoping to eventually be accepted into postgraduate study with a view to helping people experiencing post-traumatic stress disorder, or children experiencing procedural anxiety due to prolonged and ongoing medical conditions.

Overall, I believe that I have achieved every one of my mum's dreams for me and I wish she were here to see my accomplishments. I am living the fulfilled life that she hoped I would have, and more. I am raising awareness within the general community about people with disabilities. It is a constant fight to push through society's negative assumptions about what people with disability can achieve, but I am pushing back with my own determination and actions. From the little girl not expected to even walk or achieve very much at all, I have proved them wrong.

I have recovered from serious surgery, attended mainstream schooling, met that someone special, learned to walk so that I could surprise people on my wedding day and gone on to enjoy married life. Additionally, I now have a university education goal before me that I am passionate about achieving.

My philosophy on life is that if I can dream it, I can achieve it. A philosophy that my mum held close to her heart when she dreamed big dreams for me. My life's journey is now going far beyond my mum's dreams. I have emerged from her shadow, a strong and determined woman crafting her own destiny and believing that life can be extraordinary. There is so much more for me to see, experience and accomplish. I will do it all!

TWENTY-THREE

My Life with Huntington's Disease

by Ben Wilson

It's my privilege to share with you some aspects of my life's journey in this book, and to show how having the disability of Huntington's disease, doesn't necessarily mean inability. In fact, I will provide the science of positive psychology which is behind the strategies I've used to thrive with it.

My life is dominated by, but not defined by, Huntington's Disease. HD is a genetic brain disorder that causes people to lose the ability to walk, talk, think and reason over the course of ten to twenty years.

It's like having Parkinson's, Alzheimer's, Dementia, Bipolar and ALS (Lou Gehrig's) all at the same time but it is complicated by the fact that it presents differently for everyone.

The disease is also known as Huntington's Chorea. Chorea is a Latin word meaning 'to dance', so watch out for me on the dance floor. I'm dangerous!

When addressing people in public, I request to speak early in the event. It's important I speak before I have a drink because I don't want to slur my words any more than someone with HD typically does!

Seriously though, it's not uncommon for people with HD to be mistaken for being intoxicated by security and police when in public; yet another example of the misunderstanding at best, and hostility at worst that many in our community face.

This is part of my motivation for becoming an HD advocate—to change perceptions, to increase awareness and to encourage a real desire to understand others, rather than to fear them.

I decided to have the test for the disease at Flinders Hospital at twenty-four years of age. Counselling occurs beforehand to prepare people for the worst because a positive result could result in despair and increases the risk of self-harm. Only 13% of potential candidates for HD have the test because most are in denial, which is a common coping mechanism. The odds of having HD are like the toss of a coin or 50/50.

I lost the toss.

People with HD wait for years until symptoms show, which for me was not until I was in my late thirties. Symptom hunting occurs often, and I also made comparisons with my father to see where he was at the same stage of his life as me.

There are a few effective treatments that mask the symptoms. Antidepressants can help with mood and can prolong proper brain function.

A cure, however, has remained elusive.

Disability strikes wider than just the individual. Spare a thought for my nan who lost her entire immediate family to HD: my father, uncle and grandfather. Generations of anguish.

I feel blessed to know that she lived to see our two children born without HD because we had PGD (pre-implantation genetic diagnosis) through the in vitro fertilisation (IVF) process. This hereditary disease in the Wilson family dies with me.

IVF is a very costly exercise (over $50k about ten years ago), and I feel for couples who find themselves in the predicament of wanting this as an option but cannot afford it. The benefits of having children this way outweigh the costs.

Living with HD requires a committed and determined support network: GPs, neurologists, psychiatrists, psychologists, social workers and carers. I use a chiropractor to treat injuries from involuntary movements and receive remedial massage and acupuncture. Diet needs to be high in protein as I can use up to 5,000 calories a day. Good sleep is crucial, as is staying healthy and avoiding illness. Mineral spas can provide great relief.

You need to be a self-funded retiree by age forty because people with HD normally don't work beyond that age. I've just turned forty myself, and I'm a long way from that.

It's difficult to come to terms with your own mortality and the inevitability of early death. Many health professionals that I have seen fall into a fixed mindset, because they believe that with HD your genetic fate is predetermined and there is nothing you can do about it. Instead, I chose to find opportunities to grow, to develop, to learn from errors, to be resilient in the face of adversity.

I refuse to let HD force me to sit in a corner, robbed of vitality, waiting meekly for the end.

Dylan Thomas wrote, 'Do not go gentle into that good night ...' Huntington's can slowly take my body; it will not take my identity, my spirit.

Some years ago, I was introduced to the evidence-based approach of Positive Psychology, developed by Martin Seligman. The resilience training I completed is designed to boost your wellbeing and support others to do the same. I recommend his work to all of you and your children.

At the end of 2014, my first symptoms of involuntary movements began. Just a few months later, and coming up to our ten-year wedding anniversary, my marriage suddenly ended. I went into a downward spiral. For the next year, my resilience was tested as I withdrew from everyone and everything I loved. I battled anxiety, depression and demons of doubt and despair. I'm afraid to say I had suicidal thoughts. I stared into the abyss of post-traumatic stress syndrome.

The first strategy to get me out of the hole and to start to grow from the experience, was to use Professor Seligman's 'PERMA+', which are the pillars that underpin my approach to life. These principles are: positive emotion, engagement, relationships, meaning, achievement and health. I tried to apply these to my career in education, to get back to seeing teaching for the gift it is and going to the gym which provided an excellent outlet. It helped me socially, to stay fit, feel strong, and is good for my balance. It's hard to feel anxious and depressed about your future when you're huffing and puffing during a session.

It's important for your wellbeing to be in a 'flow state' sometimes called 'being in the zone' (the E in PERMA+), where time flies because you are completely engaged in and energised by the task at hand. I have experienced it playing and coaching sport, teaching in the classroom, at the gym, playing/listening to music, surfing and more recently speaking to groups. People who are ill or in pain report that their symptoms abate or go away completely in a flow state.

The other strategy was to take a strengths-based approach; knowing and applying your strengths is another formula that is also very useful. My top character strengths are spirituality and gratitude. These were used when doing a powerful prayer and meditation that I read about in a book (*Breaking the Habit of Being Yourself* by Joe Dispenza) that involved visualising about my preferred self. It talks about the importance of gratitude and how there is no room for anxiety, fear, anger and depression where love, joy and gratitude exist. I'm certain that it was someone's (God's) plan to have the book recommended to me at a time when I needed it most.

It ties in beautifully with my faith and gives me a ritual that helps me explore my spiritual side and get closer to God. It also says that leaders like Jesus were great because they think greater than themselves, which is something that I've tried to model.

After doing the prayer, meditation and visualisation almost on a daily basis, I noticed that my life started to change, and new opportunities opened up. I've been blessed every step of the way, especially after the decision to open up and come out about my HD.

It's been a secret in families for generations, and that must change. I would encourage people to do the same but to carefully consider when the time is right for you. I discussed it with a colleague and friend, while having breakfast on holidays at Bombora's Café Goolwa Beach. His advice was that, ultimately, I had two choices: one was to stay in the closet so to speak, and the other was to do something about it, share my story, be a role model to my children and leave a legacy. When put like that what choice did I have?

People say, they are blessed to have the disease and I have been blessed to meet my partner Melanie and am grateful for her patience and love. I know that I make great demands on her and can be both physically and emotionally clumsy. I cherish every moment of our life together, and it's a privilege to have co-founded 'Hope HD' with her.

I also became an Ambassador for Huntington's South Australia and Northern Territory.

In both roles, I have set myself a goal to raise awareness, and bring a message of hope to the community—that people can still flourish despite dealing with one of the most debilitating diseases known to humankind.

I was endorsed as the Dignity Party candidate for Dunstan in the State Election in March 2018.

I was also asked to make a documentary for Collingwood Football Club's website that shows the human side of past players (yes, how things have changed!) and to contribute to this book, by showing that disability doesn't necessarily mean inability.

Finally, we are seeing the first positive development of a cure for HD in trials, that has not only slowed the progression of the illness but could potentially reverse it as well.

I strongly believe that it is important to focus on solutions to problems rather than just to complain, an attitude I'd describe as 'It's better to light a candle than to curse the darkness.' I also understand that many people have good intentions, however, they put things off.

When I was at school, I read this quote from Etienne de Grellet who said:

'I expect to pass through this world but once; any good thing therefore that I can do, or any kindness that I can show to any fellow creature, let me do it now; let me not defer or neglect it, for I shall not pass this way again.'[16]

I have adopted this as my personal mantra.

I speak for those with HD, who need support and understanding, who need equality of opportunity, who have no voice of their own. I aspire to be someone who helps people to help themselves, a shoulder to lean on, a listener and a doer.

My disability of living with Huntington's disease doesn't necessarily mean living with inability. With the assistance of the positive psychology framework, I have continued to strive towards my goals and flourish despite my condition. My evolving story is how, with the love and friendship of many, post-traumatic stress in my life was transformed into post-traumatic growth and hope, acute self-awareness and a passionate desire to serve others. I urge you all to live in the moment, to find your best self, to grow in all your relationships and support this book.

Here's to DisAbility 'lighting a candle on the darkness.'
website: www.hopehd.com
Facebook: hope HD
Twitter: @BenWillo77
Instagram: hopeHD
Further reading:
https://www.wellbeingandresilience.com/sites/swrc5/media/pdf/permaandcentreoverview.pdf accessed 25 Feb 2019

---

16 http://www.quotationspage.com/quote/29212.html

TWENTY-FOUR

Redlegs and Family

by Rick Neagle and Marie Doerner

Growing up, football was everything. I had wanted to play for the Norwood Football Club aka 'the Redlegs' for as long as I could remember. And amazingly, my dreams came true. The hard work, long practices, a bit of luck and a lot of dedication all paid off. Soon I was playing professionally, and I loved it. There was nothing as invigorating as being on the oval. Nothing felt as great as competing for the ball, kicking goals and winning matches. Sure, there were losses. Sure, there was the recuperation. Nursing the body so it was ready to go into the battle next week and the week after that.

But each week the recovery took longer. The pain lasted just a few more hours, then days and then not at all. Eventually, I was diagnosed with mitochondrial myopathy: the energy-producers in my muscle cells were not working; my muscles were not regenerating; they didn't have the energy. No worries. My career had spanned five years, 66 league games, 84 goals. So I took on another role for the Redlegs, as physiotherapist.

Now it was time to focus on my new career and my personal life. I set up a sports physiotherapy practice with my partners at Wakefield Sports Clinic, got married and started a family. First came Taylah, the light of my life, and then Mitchell, a beacon to the meaning of my life. Life was great.

But something was not right. It was hard to put a finger on it. Mitchell was not like other children. At two years old, the doctor reassured me that everything was fine and she discounted my concern. We were in a good space in Dulwich. It was a great neighbourhood with trees and good people. I tried to develop a peaceful existence by practising yoga, acupuncture, spinal manipulation and continuing with my work as an APA sports physiotherapist with the Redlegs.

By the time Mitchell was three, his symptoms were worse. He ate things that were not food ('pica' behaviours), didn't connect with or learn like other children. Finally I found Professor Robyn Young, an expert in autism and its consequences, and she made the diagnosis of autism. That was the beginning of a long road ahead. Mitchell had lost valuable time. Therapies and treatments were available, but we should have started earlier. Trying to find help for Mitchell was slow and frustrating. This was a new battle. The Redlegs had taught me how to fight and fight I did.

Unfortunately, as is the case with many other families coping with disabilities and doctors and difficult diagnoses, my marriage dissolved. Taking care of Mitchell and finding care for him was exhausting, leaving only suffering in my marital relationship. However, Mitchell was not to blame. In fact, he was a gift showing me the way out of what was a dysfunctional, bad marriage to his mother. Also there was Taylah, beautiful Taylah. So much energy went into her little brother that she often lost out. I worked hard to make sure she was able to enjoy a typical childhood and grow to be herself. To know that she, too, was important.

Finally the emotional strain in the family was all too much. Working as a physiotherapist had taken its toll on my body. The physical strain on my body from my muscle disease made the decision for me to retire from paid work and put all my effort into being Mitchell's primary carer and more importantly, a present father. Now I could take him to therapy after therapy. Before taking on a role as his primary carer, I had previously found a program called 'Applied Behaviour Therapy', or ABA. While this created a financial strain, costing $50,000 a year, Mitchell made sound progress. I was shocked to find how little support was out there for people with autism. Yes, there were good doctors and programs, but they took money, time and energy.

By 2004, my frustration with the political system and support systems for people with disabilities reached a peak. A group of other parents also shared these frustrations. What was going to happen to our kids as they grew? It was hard enough to find schools and programs that were adequate for our children while they were small. What would happen when our kids grew up? Would they work? Where would they get services? Where were the services? Where would he live when I wasn't around anymore?

It was time to start a new battle. It was time for a new fight. Together, we established a political party, the 'Dignity for Disabled Party' (d4d).[17] We wanted to lobby parliament for increased funding for people with disabilities. We went to the media and tried to raise awareness of the issues that people with disabilities face. Our funding was the 'smell of an oily rag', but we did not

---

17   https://dignityparty.org.au

give up. In 2009, we changed the name to 'Dignity for Disability'. We discovered that words are important. There were many people in the community who bristled at the word 'disabled'. A disabled car is a car that cannot work; a car with defects or parts that were removed. Saying, a 'disabled person' does not make sense. A person with a disability is a person first. They live with a disability. They still have abilities. Every person on the planet deserves to dignity so d4d became Dignity for Disability. Better words and a better focus. Passion was reignited. This was a human rights issue. We expanded the scope of our mission to include support for mental health and increased our party membership. Systemic change was upon us and it was cathartic.

In 2010, we had seven party members stand for election and Kelly Vincent was elected on the back of some extraordinary circumstances. Coming up to the election the d4d's lead candidate, Dr Paul Collier was eager to serve. He had firsthand knowledge of disability. On the way to his twenty-first birthday celebration, Paul was involved in a car accident which damaged his spine leading to quadriplegia—paralysis of his legs and lower body, plus impairment of his arms and hands. By 2010, he was ready to shift the bar to ensure that people with disabilities were served by their government. Then suddenly, Paul suffered a massive stroke and died a few days later, just eleven days before the election. This caused an enormous media and press flurry. d4d received an inordinate amount of coverage and the word was out. During the election, many people still voted for Paul and others voted for Kelly Vincent. Since only live candidates can receive votes, all of Paul's votes went to Kelly. A primary vote of 1.3% at the ballot box, meant that Kelly ended up with an upper house seat with 11% of the vote after preferences. At twenty-one, her first job was as a member of parliament.

In 2016, the name was shortened to the 'Dignity Party'. The mission was broadened to represent equality of all forms: including race, gender, age and sexual orientation. We were working hard and making progress. We knew that there was a better way to serve people; that it was necessary and possible. Interest in the movement spread across Australia and people from all over the world started asking questions.

There needs to be a greater awareness around disability. Until it strikes your family, many people don't realise how little support is out there. Disability can happen anywhere, to anyone, at any time. People with disabilities live in all our neighbourhoods. Their needs are often invisible to the general public.

Laws are needed to ensure equity. We fought long and hard, lobbying the government of the day, and in particular the Attorney General, to introduce a raft of legislative changes under the umbrella of what we called the 'Disability Justice Plan'. This work brought extra funding, new laws and improved human rights for people with the lived experience of disability; essentially, those that care for and support people with a disability.

The wider public has been put on notice that those who abuse vulnerable people can be imprisoned. However, there is still a long way to go. We hope that the Royal Commission into the Abuse of People with Disabilities will lift the cloak of abuse, stop it and hold abusers accountable for their actions.

The Dignity Party introduced laws around universal design. Improving accessibility is needed to ensure equity. Focusing on the principles of universal design, we have been working on some small but powerful things like universal pathways and universal amphibious sun lounges, so the beaches become accessible to people with disabilities. All houses and institutions and businesses should be designed to meet the needs of everyone. Remember when door handles were all round? Young strong hands could easily open the doors. But what if your arms are filled with groceries? What if you have no hands? What if holding your child takes both hands? The new lever-type doorhandles can be opened with an elbow, with your wrist. A simple design change means many more people can walk through that door. Children need access from birth; adults need access till death. It makes a lot of sense and does not cost much. It is a human right that all people have equal and equitable access to mainstream services and public spaces.

The 'Count Me In Foundation'[18] has continued the great work of promoting awareness and implementing universal design, building on the foundations that were put in place by the Dignity Party. Count Me In is a not-for-profit organisation operating in South Australia, founded and majority-managed by people with disability. We believe that by including people with a disability and their carers in the management, design and delivery of universal design principles in public places and buildings, we will create a better and more participant-driven community. The foundation is trying to give children and adults with disabilities access to South Australia. Count Me In's corporate partners, Total Beach Access,[19] has signed a binding contract with the United Nations to supply its products (Universal Walkways and Amphibious Sun Lounges) to 3800 'United Nations Blue Flag' accredited beaches all around the world. These mechanisms are expensive but change the lives of all people. Now people with wheelchairs can travel on the beach mat along the beach, but so can parents with small children in pushers. Many people have commented on how user-friendly the mats are. They make the world better for all.

---

18 https://www.countmein.com.au
19 https://totalbeachaccess.com/

Today the journey continues. Mitchell wants to be like other young men his own age. He wants a job, his own home, his independence. Although Mitchell is a beautiful kid, he can also be a danger to himself. It takes a team of workers to keep him on the right track. I try to see him every day. Over the years, he has gathered more diagnoses—anxiety disorder, bipolar disorder. Any small change can activate his anxiety. He depends on funding.

Taylah is growing to be a wonderful young woman who is studying psychology. She volunteers and has run for parliament as a member of the Dignity Party. She has great skills and her emotional intelligence is second to none.

Fatherhood has been a wonderfully rewarding experience. It has taken me to unexpected places. I believe it is more important to know some of the questions than all of the answers. I don't know all the answers—I still have many, many questions though. I believe I am a social capitalist or a capital socialist; I am not sure. However, one thing that I am certain of is that being involved in my community both politically and socio-economically is very important. We have to find good solutions for people with disabilities. They should have the right to be part of the community. They should not have to spend all their energy finding and funding their very existence. My work as an activist has just started.

TWENTY-FIVE

Losing Sight, Gaining Insight

by Nadja Fernandes

IN 1989 GORDON,[20] THEN TWENTY-ONE YEARS OF AGE, WAS AT the pub with his younger brother, Stephen, on a Saturday night. They were in a joyful mood and spontaneously started a little game that ended up as a prank. They started pretending to communicate in Auslan. As they had not previously established who was supposed to be the one with a hearing disability, they kept making gestures in a way that anyone observing would actually believe at least one of the two brothers was indeed deaf—anyone except of course someone who was proficient in Auslan.

---

20 This is not his real name.

A few minutes later, a young girl approached them, and Stephen greeted her. Most likely due to their physical resemblance, she correctly assumed they were brothers.

Hi. Is that your brother? she asked as she smiled at both of them.

... Yep.
... Is he deaf?
... He is.
... I think he's cute.

Stephen turned to face Gordon and made some random gestures, pretending to the girl that he was telling Gordon in Auslan that the girl thought he was cute. Gordon 'replied' with some gestures of his own, and then Stephen faced the girl again and announced: 'He thinks you're cute too!'

At this moment, Gordon's eyes popped out, and he moved so that his brother could see him, but the girl could not. With a facial expression that clearly expressed his annoyance, he started shaking his head vigorously. Meanwhile, the other two continued the dialogue:

... What's his favourite drink?
... He likes Kahlua and milk.

Gordon's eyes opened even wider, if that was possible. This time he shook his head and waved his arms in a crossing movement indicating a clear and loud 'NO'.

Gordon ended up drinking Kahlua and milk and was deprived of speaking for a good hour. His brother, on the other hand, had a great time and had to make a gigantic effort not to laugh so as not to give away their prank. The girl asked many questions, and said she thought it was so sweet of Stephen to take Gordon out, and that it was so cool they were so close, and blah-blah-blah.

Three or four drinks later, both brothers were out of the pub, both laughing their heads off. Gordon was not deaf, although he may have suffered some hearing loss only around a year before that, when he had stayed 'home alone' while his family took a trip to New York. As he still lived at home, being on his own felt like a dream! You know what they say, 'when the cat is away, ...' So, when Gordon's parents returned, they found empty champagne and wine glasses in the garden and the bathrooms, and they also found that their stereo speakers had been burst.

Some twelve months later, in 1989, when Gordon was playing a practical joke together with his brother, in a 'make believe I'm deaf' stunt, he did not imagine that he would, in the not so distant future, lose his sight almost entirely.

~

Gordon once lived and worked in the south west, in a vineyard. His days used to start at the crack of dawn, and Gordon would be up with the first cock's crow. A copper kettle would be sitting on his gas stovetop and his dog, Magnum, at his feet, would be wagging his tail, excited about going out into the wild, where he, like his master, saw no boundaries.

By the end of the day, Gordon had driven a tractor, sprayed some leaves, pruned the grape vines, supervised the work of other staff, hired new staff, and paid them. Interestingly, he had recruited a totally deaf person, another worker with a less severe hearing disability, and someone 'legally blind'—although this was before Gordon lost his sight.

Despite the repetitive nature of the job, he believed being outdoors made it all worthwhile. Every ten days of work or so, he'd come to Perth and spend a few days at his second home, where his wife lived and worked.

'I miss that rural lifestyle. I actually make more money nowadays, but I much preferred working in the bush', he says these days.

Although his father held two university degrees, Gordon was never much of an academic, and was never pressured into doing something he did not like. He started uni, twice, and apparently, was kicked out, twice.

'I wasn't forced to go to uni but was encouraged to try and see if I liked. So, I chose to study agriculture. I guess in hindsight, no pun intended, I knew I wanted to be outdoors, in the bush. But while at uni, the pub was so much more attractive!'

Gordon had become aware that his vision was not good. His eyesight had deteriorated to such an extent that he was no longer able to spray the leaves in the vineyard, and most other duties became next to impossible to him, and eventually he had to resign from his job in the bush and come back to the so-called 'big city'. He left his little dwelling behind and moved permanently to Perth.

Upon arriving in Perth, he had an eye test done. The result stated that he only had approximately 10% of his vision and his driver's licence was confiscated. His condition is called Retinitis Pigmentosa, commonly known as RP, a genetic degenerative disease where the typical early symptom is the loss of night sight. Gordon had, in fact, been diagnosed many years before and had stopped driving at night prior to having to quit his job; but for a while, he still had enough sight during the day to carry out his usual activities without difficulty. His sight loss happened gradually until one day he realised his vision was just not enough for him to keep fulfilling all the duties which his job required.

But Gordon is not the kind of guy who is looking for sympathy. There is no self-pity in his words nor in his attitude. Although he does not try to make it as if it was nothing, he is also lucid and objective enough to recognise his good fortune in other areas of his life. I think after having met him, that was one of the things I learned: to focus more on the tools and favourable conditions I have, and try to make something out of that, rather than looking at what I don't have and letting that determine my fate. Gordon goes one step further than me because he adds humour to his philosophy. He'll say for instance, 'When they made me give up my licence, I started riding my pushbike', and he laughs. It's true: he rode his bike to the local shops for a few months, until his family decided to take his bike away, for his own sake.

My daughter, who is now in Year Six, has known him since she can remember. She has learned to guide him when we go out with such prowess that it would put some grownups to shame. I read a short story once, fictional, in which the main character was a blind man. I think the fact that there was a blind person in the story aroused my curiosity and interest, given my direct involvement with Gordon. The story was very well written and insightful. Its one flaw was that this blind man, who was the main character, was described as being pulled by the hand by a friend who was guiding him. The first thing I learned about assisting visually impaired people when I met Gordon, was that ideally, the visually-impaired person holds the guide's arm with one hand and then tries to follow the guide's movements and direction. The guide's arm functions a bit like a steering wheel, determining which way the guided person goes. So, my daughter learned to guide him well. She is so used to doing so many things with him—from building sand castles, to wrestling, to watching kids' TV shows together. As a result, more than once they walked to the local ice-cream shop and after finishing their ice-cream (bear in mind that I was not with them), she walked out of the place without him. She was expecting him to follow behind, only to realise, as she reached the first corner, that he was still at the shop, waiting to be guided. I take it she does not see him as blind ... that's probably partly because he lives a life that looks to her so active, unlike what some people would imagine for someone with any disability.

Gordon has a wicked sense of humour and never misses a chance to make a joke, no matter at the expense of whom, even if it's his own. Over twenty years after pretending to be deaf with his brother, pranks are still appealing to him, and my daughter has played a few on me, at his instructions. Once I left my car parked in his driveway and walked to the University of Western Australia, where I was working at the time. I had been doing that for over a week, as there was no parking available on campus, and Gordon had offered for me to leave my car there. Around 2:30 pm, as I was walking back to my car, I saw a piece of paper on my windscreen. My heart started to beat faster, and inside my head I said, *No! They can't give me a fine! I'm not parked on the street.* As I reached my car, I picked up the piece of paper and read, 'This is a fine from the City of Nedlands. Hahaha! I pranked you! Crazy Gordon.' I then imagined him laughing by himself, inside his own place. My daughter thinks he has a cheeky smile. Once she saw one of his early school photos and spotted him amongst the other children. When I queried her about how she realised which one he was, her reply was, 'Well, he still has the same cheeky smile.'

Around 2004 he suffered another episode of major sight deterioration. It was around the same time he broke up with his partner, and also lost his four-legged companion, Magnum, who had to be put to sleep. Gordon dropped into a dark hole, but not for long. At the invitation of his dad, he did a course called Landmark Forum where he learned life skills—whatever that means ... Then he became acquainted with the Association for the Blind, where he got involved with different types of training. He tried to learn Braille but abandoned it shortly after learning the basics, as he thought it was too complicated, and he felt it did not fulfil many of his personal needs. It did not have enough value for him personally, as it made little difference in his daily life.

Gordon and I met around eight years ago, on social media. 'Mmmm,' can I hear you say, 'What? Social media? A blind guy using social media?' Yes, you read it correctly. He has been using a computer for over a decade. He probably uses it a lot more these days, after losing his sight, than when he could still see. His computer magnifies the fonts. Remember he still has 1% of his vision. I personally cannot comprehend what that actually means but it cannot be much. He explained it to me that he can see shapes and shadows, and if there is enough contrast in colour, depending on the light, he can see a bit better. For instance, sometimes, if he stares at the table number in a restaurant, the ones that are printed on a white squarish shaped card, held by a stand, with black fonts, he can often tell the number. However, that would be very limiting, as far as using a computer goes. This is why his computer also reads his texts to him. If he receives an email, he can have it read to him. To reply, he still needs to type.

He did find much more value in golf lessons for visually impaired people. When I had just met him, I remember how amazing I thought it was to have a blind friend who could play golf well and had only learned it after he'd lost his sight. I asked Gordon if he was into sport before losing his sight and he said he enjoyed swimming, and water sports in general. He had even done the Perth-to-Rottnest swimming race once, with his brother, Stephen. *Impressive*, I thought to myself when I heard the story.

'Can you think of any way in which you believe your life has changed for the better?' I asked him once. He twisted his lips a bit and looked up, as if trying to access his own hard-drive. Then he told me some incredible stories about his youth days. After listening, I labelled him a complete and ruthless daredevil. Then I said to him, 'You know, I'm starting to believe in God. I think God might have made you blind to save your life. If you had not lost your sight, you might have lost your life.' He chuckled and replied, 'You're probably right! D'you wanna beer?'

One of the many trainings Gordon did after losing his sight was a course on options and shares trading. Not only did he learn enough about that, but he actually earns a living trading options on the Stock Market. Day in, day out, Gordon gets up around an hour before the market opens, makes himself a coffee, has some breakfast, then 'goes to work'. For him, it's only a few steps, as his office is next door to his bedroom. Still impressive, since most people I know who work from home find it hard to have enough discipline to do it in a structured way. Gordon does it every day, without his eyesight. He sits in front of the computer, consults the internet to check the share prices, their falls and rises, and he manages to make the market work for him. 'You must be so good,' I say to him. Again, he laughs, then tells me, 'You have to be humble when you're trading. As soon as you think you're good, that's when you make a mistake and are reminded you aren't. The first month I traded options, I made $15,000. I thought I was a genius. The second month I lost $10,000. I started to doubt my skills ... By the fourth month I had broken even.' He says all this in a genuinely cheerful tone. I realise he has become a real trader. *It must be the daredevil in him again*, I tell myself. He admits he enjoys the risk factor and tells me that it's not possible to always win, but with time you learn to minimise your losses.

The first time I took him for a ride in my car I actually thought that he was pranking me, pretending to be blind—and I did not even know yet about the deaf prank he and Stephen had played.

We drove to a cafe not far from his place. Rather than giving me the address, he directed me, almost street by street, telling me where to turn left, where to turn right, and even where to park. I asked him how he knew all that and he said he'd lived in the area for a long time ... I decided to take him somewhere else, a bit further, to a different suburb. I told him we'd be going to Leederville because I wanted him to try a special hot chocolate at a special cafe. He accepted my invitation, and we both got into my car. When I was two minutes from my destination, he asked me if we were on Oxford Street. Do I need to say he was right? I don't think so. Again, I asked him how he knew where we were. 'I worked as a driver many years ago, and I had to learn my way around everywhere. These days because I can't see, I reckon I pay even more attention, without even thinking about it.' To make it more disconcerting for me, many times, while driving, I took the wrong turn, and as soon as that happened, Gordon inquired, 'Where are you going?' or 'Shouldn't you have turned just then?'

We get together quite often, and I'm so used to his company that sometimes when we're out shopping it almost feels like I'm his eyes: I start telling him about everything I can see that is interesting. Half the time he decides to buy something he hadn't planned to, but after hearing the description I provide him, he can't resist the temptation. Most of the time it is food, but once he ended up buying a $300 vintage-look state-of-the-art digital radio, with Bluetooth connection. A few weeks later he was wondering why he had bought it when he already owned a radio. 'Sorry, mate. I'll try to shut up and talk less,' I say to him. He replies, 'That's fine. It doesn't bother me as much as some of the music you listen to, which has made me wish a few times I had a hearing disability instead of a visual.'

There is a general assumption that when a person has lost part or all of one of the five senses, they tend to have the other ones more acutely developed; it seems to be true. Gordon can smell smoke every time there is some controlled burning. When we walk to the shops, he'll also comment on different smells, such as hair products—and somehow, I look around and see there is a new hair salon that opened, or the food people are eating. 'Smell the petrichor,' he said another time, as we walked out one summer morning after a bit of rain. My favourite anecdote has to be when once I was waiting for him in his kitchen while he finished some work in his office, which is upstairs. All of a sudden I heard, 'Oy! Stop eating my blueberries!'

'How do you know?' I asked in surprise, to which he laughed and told me he knows all the sounds produced in his house.

In 2010 Gordon went to Canada for six weeks with Stephen. While on the plane, he befriended an air hostess, and they have since met many times, and he even visited her in her home country, in South East Asia. When he first told me the story about how they met, I couldn't help asking, 'How did that happen?' To which he replied, 'Obviously, I do my best work forty thousand feet above the ground', and he grinned. That cheeky smile, as my daughter often puts it.

FUNDRAISING

Did you enjoy the book?
Are you in the need to raise funds for
your organisations (or yourself)?
If the answers are **yes** and **yes**, please
visit our Fundraising page.
eighteenpointfive.com.au/fundraising
We can deliver books to you in Australia
for as low as $9.70 a book*.

(* The cost varies with the number of books ordered.
Visit our website for the latest information and prices)

THANK YOU

Eighteen Point Five Pty Ltd would like to thank the following people and organisations.

Project Management
John Duthie

Editing
Beverley Streater (book)
Katie Webb (blogs)

Contributions and writing (additional writing)
Alex (Nadja Fernandes)
Alice Waterman (SACARE Adelaide)
Bee Williamson
Ben Wilson
Faisal Rusdi & Cucu Rusdi (Marie Doerner)
Gail Miller
Gordon Smart (Nadja Fernandes)
Grant Lock
Jacy Arthur (Diana von der Borch-Garden)
James, Cristina & Kym Rodert (Marie Doerner)
John Duthie
John Rynn (Judith Buckinham)
Jonathan Nguyen (Chantel Bongiovanni)
Kathryn Hall (Rachel Mann)
Linda Fistonich (Valerie Everett)
Mary Albury (Valerie Everett)
Melinda Jones (David Wayne Wilson)
Michael & Kathleen Kuhn (May-Kuan Lim)
Nessa Vlajkovic

Neville Hiatt
Phillippa Smoker
Rick & Mitchell Neagle (Marie Doerner)
Ross Hill-Brown (John Francis)
Tracey Meg (May-Kuan Lim)
Zia Westerman (Pam Farley)

Proofreading
John Duthie
Lisa Birch
Lorraine Saunders
Marie Doerner
Rachel Mann
Zia Westerman

Supporters
Access2Arts
Adelaide Unicare
BookPOD
Bridgett McDonald
Byron Writers Festival
Cara
Caring Clothing
Christian Professional Writers SA
Dignity Party
Immersion Therapy™
Independent Living Centre TAS
Karen Brown
Lane Slagle Starfish Education
Lyn Yeowart
Maribel Steel

Marion Writers Group
Messenger Newspapers
Natalie Oliveri Music Therapy
PQSA Paraquad South Australia
Prostek
Rise Church Northgate
SA Writers Centre Inc
SACARE Adelaide
Se.care
Spartacus Duthie
Sylvie Blair
The Department for Communities and Social Inclusion
The KSP Writers Centre
The Lifetime Support Authority
The NSW Writers Centre
The NT Writers Centre
The Society of Women Writers
Vision Australia Radio
Whyalla Writers Group
YWCA Australia

www.ingramcontent.com/pod-product-compliance
Lightning Source LLC
Chambersburg PA
CBHW050306010526
44107CB00055B/2117